THEORY AND RELIGIOUS UNDERSTANDING:

A CRITIQUE OF THE HERMENEUTICS OF JOACHIM WACH

THEORY AND RELIGIOUS UNDERSTANDING:

A CRITIQUE OF THE HERMENEUTICS OF JOACHIM WACH

by

Charles Monroe Wood

Published by

AMERICAN ACADEMY OF RELIGION

and

SCHOLARS PRESS

AAR DISSERTATION SERIES, NUMBER 12

1975

Distributed by

SCHOLARS PRESS
University of Montana
Missoula, Montana 59801

THEORY AND RELIGIOUS UNDERSTANDING:
A CRITIQUE OF THE HERMENEUTICS OF JOACHIM WACH

by

Charles Monroe Wood

Ph.D., 1972   Advisor:
Yale University   Hans Frei

Library of Congress Cataloging in Publication Data

Wood, Charles Monroe.
    Theory and religious understanding.

    (AAR dissertation series ; 12)
    Originally presented as the author's thesis, Yale,
1972.
    Bibliography: p.
    1. Religion--Historiography--History. 2. Her-
meneutics--History. 3. Wach, Joachim, 1898-1955.
I. Title. II. Series: American Academy of Re-
ligion. Dissertation series - American Academy of
Religion ; 12.
BL41.W58 1975   200'.1   75-26839
ISBN 0-89130-026-0

Printed in the United States of America

Printing Department
University of Montana
Missoula, Montana 59801

CONTENTS

CHAPTER I

FREEDOM AND FAITHFULNESS IN UNDERSTANDING

"Unless you believe, surely you will not understand," runs
the Septuagint text of Isaiah 7:9. This verse--an influential
mistranslation--has been cited throughout Christian history to
warrant theological determination of the correct approach to
the interpretation of Scripture and doctrine. It is one of the
earlier, and stronger, instances of what has come to be called
"the hermeneutical circle," the principle that no understanding
is possible without some sort of prior grasp of that which is
to be understood.

Echoes of Isaiah 7:9 can be heard at some distance from
this theological neighborhood. They can be detected, for example, in the popular conviction that any religion can be truly
understood only by its adherents: assent is the only road to
comprehension. The outsider is, by that very status, never in
a position to claim that he understands, and hence never com-
petent to criticize the religious life or doctrine of a group.
This line of thought extends beyond the issue of religious understanding, of course. It reaches an extreme in a sort of
individualistic relativism: no one can ever really understand
another person at all, since no one can fully share the complex
of experience and thought in which another lives.

The phrase, "really understand," often encountered in such
claims, is in any case a signal that the definition of "understanding" itself may be at issue. Is it to be a synonym for
sympathy, for agreement, or even for identity? Perhaps a person who defines it so is simply refusing to concede that anyone
could "really understand" his position and remain unconvinced.
Or perhaps he feels alienated ("misunderstood," as we sometimes
say), and wishes for the kind of understanding which brings
reconciliation and wholeness.

But the claim that understanding requires assent cannot be
entirely dismissed or discredited by such hypotheses regarding

the motives of its proponents. For it may also be heard as a
legitimate protest against the misuse of the concept of "understanding." The human desire for mastery (an old synonym for
"understanding"), for autonomy and control, and the consequent
tendency to manipulate things and people from a distance rather
than to come close and listen and risk a relationship, is well
known. The theologians' frequent stipulation that a reader
must humble himself and approach the Scriptures attentively,
rather than set himself as their capable critic and judge, is
rooted in this knowledge. The theme has been generalized and
given popular currency in the existentialist equation of objectivity with inauthenticity, in the demand for *engagement*
rather than distance and detachment in the search for truth.
If "subjectivity is truth," then whatever is attained by "objectivity" and cool impartiality cannot be true understanding.
Understanding must involve existential participation; if the
interpreter holds himself back from this total involvement, he
will not be able to render more than a reductionist explanation
of that which he seeks to understand.

By taking this course, the protest against misappropri-
ations of the concept of "understanding" finds itself allied
with certain accounts of the nature of the process of understanding as such--accounts which weld understanding to participation and decision and which deny the possibility of an
understanding which incorporates objective knowledge and judgment. Such an account is operative, for example, in the hermeneutics of Rudolf Bultmann. "To understand history," he
writes, "is possible only for one who does not stand over
against it as a neutral, non-participating observer, but himself stands in history and shares responsibility for it."
Understanding is possible only where there is an "*existentiell*
encounter," where the interpreter acknowledges his own life-
relationship to the concerns expressed directly or indirectly
in the text, and is thus open to the influence of the text.[1]
What is "understood" in such an encounter is not an object,
but a new range of possibilities for one's own existence; there
is therefore no room for objective criticism, but only for decision. "In the text," says Bultmann, "the exegete encounters
a claim, i.e. is there offered a self-understanding that he
can accept (permit to be given to him) or reject, and is

therefore faced with the demand for decision. Even in the case
of a no, however, the understanding is a legitimate one, i.e.
is a genuine answer to the question of the text, which is not
to be refuted by argument because it is an *existentiell* decision."[2]

For Bultmann, this understanding might nevertheless be
called "objective," in the sense that any methodically gained
knowledge is objective. The existential approach is not chosen
or determined by the arbitrary demand or whim of the reader,
but instead "arises from history itself." It is uniquely suited to the task, since it is the only route to an understanding
of what the text really has to say to us.[3]

Such an approach to the nature of understanding is pressed
further by Hans-Georg Gadamer, Bultmann's sometime colleague
and the philosopher-in-residence of the "new hermeneutic."
Building from the ontology of the later Heidegger, Gadamer
views "understanding" not as one among man's various abilties
or forms of behavior, but as man's very mode of being. Understanding is never just the relation of a subject of a given
object, but rather a conscious living relationship to the
historical process which sustains both "object" and "subject,"
and thus to the Being to which both belong. We have no access
to the object as such. Its "meaning" for us is to be found at
the intersection of our world or horizon with its own, that is,
with the tradition or historical effect which it has produced
and by virtue of which it already belongs to our world. These
two worlds, whose horizons meet in understanding, make up the
"hermeneutic universe." The absence of objective reference
here is not to be lamented. Gadamer's primary hermeneutical
model is an aesthetic one, and just as "the *mens auctoris* is
no possible criterion for the meaning of a work of art," so
the meaning achieved in any understanding is not governed by
any original intention inherent in the object itself.[4] Instead, by focusing on the intersection or "fusion" of the two
horizons, we are given insight into our own present situation
and its possibilities. Understanding informs and enriches
our existence; it does not furnish knowledge about some external object, but rather brings us to an awareness of our
participation in an ongoing tradition.[5]

It is not surprising that such a treatment of understanding,

which divorces it completely from objective knowledge and
judgment but demands instead the reader's existential commitment, should find ready opponents among those concerned, for
various reasons, with the integrity of the object. Where the
object of understanding has some normative significance--in
law, for example, or perhaps even yet in theology--or where
the goal of interpretation is something other than the immediate enrichment of the interpreter's own life, there appears
to be some unwillingness to let the object be lost or discarded
in the rush for existential insight. When the protest against
positivistic or other truncated uses of "understanding" took
the form of an account of understanding which excludes objectivity, it engendered a counter-protest aimed at the recovery
of the object. Ernst Käsemann, speaking from the standpoint of
New Testament interpretation, put the situation well. In a
long note to an interpretative article, he wrote that he was
aware of the problems which can be created by the illusion that
the interpreter is the master of the object. But he continued:
"I regard the confusion of understanding and decision as no
less dangerous. The assumed compulsion of always having to
take a stand, rather than first hearing for once and waiting
for what is given or taken by that which is foreign, is usually
the death of understanding. . . . The cardinal virtue of the
historian and the beginning of all meaningful hermeneutic is
for me the practice of hearing, which begins simply by letting
what is historically foreign maintain its validity and does
not regard rape as the basic form of *engagement*."[6]

One major response which is addressed to both Bultmann
and Gadamer is that of the Italian legal historian, Emilio
Betti. He criticizes both for turning the hermeneutical conversation (that is, the interaction between subject and object)
into a soliloquy, so that it is in fact no longer an "encounter" at all. "But can such a procedure then still be called
an exposition [*Auslegung*]?", Betti asks.[7] Gadamer's approach
gives up too much. The supposed increase in self-awareness
produced by his sort of understanding does not compensate for
the surrender of objectivity. The existential treatment,
charges Betti, allows the interpreter to take from the text
whatever he finds meaningful, whatever he wishes to appropriate
for certain purposes, and to dismiss the particular character

and identity of the object as invalid.

What Betti proposes as an alternative is a return to what Joachim Wach called the "great tradition" of hermeneutics, inaugurated by Schleiermacher and revived, after the decline of speculative philosophy, by Wilhelm Dilthey. The eclipse of this tradition by the current trend in hermeneutics is regrettable, from Betti's point of view, because the hallmark of that tradition was a separation between interpretation or exposition (*Auslegung*) and the bestowal of meaning (*Sinngebung*).[8] Betti's aim in entering the hermeneutical discussion is to reaffirm that distinction as one which is still necessary and possible, and to develop canons for interpretation which will insure the autonomy of the object and control the subjective involvement of the interpreter.

This distinction and the consequent methodological principles rest expressly upon a claim common to the members of the nineteenth-century tradition to which Betti appeals: that our "historicity" is not an absolute barrier to any understanding of the object as such, but rather that subject and object share a supra-historical property or character which enables the interpreter's access to the object and permits a truly objective understanding, at least in approximation. We can discern the meaning of a strange artifact, says Betti, "because it is spirit of human spirit and (to speak with Husserl) is born of the same transcendental subjectivity."[9] The interpreter thus has a "sense" for the object; he is somehow in tune with it, has a grasp of it, prior to any actual examination. And just because of this common ground, he is able to see the object as it is, to appreciate its individuality, and to acknowledge the extent to which it is genuinely separate and different from himself.

The assumption of such a point of common identity *a priori* as the basis for understanding was developed in various forms throughout the nineteenth century. Its acceptance can be seen as the acknowledgement, by these hermeneutical theorists, of a second ancient version of the hermeneutical circle, present in pre-Socratic speculation about the *logos* and expressed classically in the Platonic doctrine of innate ideas. We understand only that which we already in some degree possess; only an inherent likeness permits receptivity. Or, as Schleiermacher observed, we may speak of understanding only with regard to that which is neither identical with us nor completely foreign to us. If it were absolutely identical, there would be no need for understanding; but if it were completely alien, we would have no access to it.[10] There must be some degree of identity, some point of contact. The consistency of Schleiermacher's hermeneutical position in this regard with his philosophical debt to Plato is not too difficult to demonstrate.[11] In a similar fashion, though with a different theoretical foundation, Dilthey attributes the possibility of understanding to the common human nature of author and reader. All individual differences are quantitative, not qualitative. They are differences of degree in the mental processes of basically similar individuals.[12] Whatever is created or expressed by one mind at any point can therefore be understood by another, since all the requisite human possibilities are universal and eternal. The reader must simply adapt his own psychical processes to correspond with those of the author to capture his intended meaning.

By accepting this form of hermeneutical circularity, and giving it appropriate theoretical support, the "great tradition" was able to maintain the distinction which Betti prizes. But there was a price. We do not need to commit ourselves existentially to the subject matter of the text in this hermeneutical procedure, but only because an agreement has already been posited generally and absolutely in the form of an *a priori* consanguinity of subject and object. We can know the object as object, and not only its particular existential significance for us, because we have already determined its possibilities in the light of the requirements of the process of understanding. Cultural artifacts, including religious documents, are accordingly not to be seen as alien phenomena. They are expressions or objectivations of the human spirit, a spirit which --by psychological similarity if not by metaphysical unity-- is everywhere and always the same.

The integrity and "objectivity" of the investigator, and the emancipation of understanding from decision or appropriation, were thus established through the prior adoption of a hypothesis concerning general human nature, and the consequent prior determination of the nature of any possible object of understanding. Whether the integrity of the object, as well as the critical freedom of the interpreter, can actually survive such a solution in any given case is at least open to question.

The questionability of the complete adequacy of Betti's alternative with its antecedents tends to support Gadamer's position. From his perspective, the object has been granted too much spurious independence already by the approach Betti wants to revive. Any such reliance on a hypothetical exemption from historicity to buttress the objectivity of understanding is simply naive. According to a supporter of Gadamer, Heinz Kimmerle, if Dilthey had been able to carry through his proposed "critique of historical reason" with genuine thoroughness, he would have discovered that any theoretical attempt (such as his own) to bridge the gap between author and reader, subject and object, was a refusal to take history seriously enough. Our radical historicity eliminates any grounds for such an assumption: there can be no bridge. Even Bultmann, says Kimmerle, indulged in unwarranted metaphysical speculation when he assumed that Heidegger's analysis of existence had a general validity and used it as a bridge between Biblical and modern existence.[13] Gadamer, however, has exposed all these false suppositions and has revealed the conditions and possibilities underlying all understanding. Gadamer himself states that he does not construct theories. He is not interested in promulgating a doctrine of interpretation which would reinforce any particular practice. He only describes the situation as it is.[14]

His description is certainly not satisfactory to Betti, with his interest in the methodology of legal interpretation; nor is it attractive to others, for whom Scripture has an objective normative value. Some of these have taken advantage of an option not available to Betti from his legal tradition. For them, Betti's appeal to the nineteenth-century theorists does not drive us back far enough. They want to explore the possibility of a return to the distinction between profane and sacred hermeneutics--a distinction Schleiermacher wanted to abolish and to replace by one between general and special hermeneutics. The former gave theologians the freedom to develop the assumptions and principles required, in their judgment, by the peculiar nature of their subject matter or by their particular interests. They were not required to submit their interpretation of Scripture to any generalized account of the nature of texts and of their possible range of meaning. In stating the necessity for a revival of the old distinction, Carl Braaten suggests that "it would seem more honest for theologians to acknowledge that in Biblical interpretation they *do* bring a preunderstanding which is conditioned by experiences and interests which are far from universally human." To admit the validity of such a preunderstanding under the name of *hermeneutica sacra* would counteract the danger of building Scriptural interpretation "on the allegedly neutral pillars of an existentialist philosophical system and the critical-historical method."[15] The prevailing general assumptions concerning the limits of understanding might in this way be parried by the acceptance of particular alternative assumptions valid for a particular case, i.e. Scripture. Something similar was advanced by Werner Schultz and directed, not against existentialist assumptions, but against Schleiermacher's general hermeneutics. His critique of Schleiermacher's dependence upon the philosophies of Plato, Spinoza and Schelling concluded with the thesis that hermeneutics should be based instead upon the Lutheran experience of justification. Schultz assumed that any form of hermeneutics must be based upon ultimate "*weltanschauliche Kategorien.*" The fundamental problem for hermeneutics, then, is to find the appropriate ones.[16]

The return to sacred hermeneutics involves, as Braaten acknowledges, a predetermination or preunderstanding of the nature of the subject matter. It is not a general, *a priori* predetermination derived from a universal theory of understanding, nor an arbitrary or whimsical predetermination by the interpreter, but one which is (it is claimed) derived from the subject matter itself and freely accepted by the interpreter as a condition for proper understanding. In this sense it is a renewed appeal to the first version of the hermeneutical circle, that of Isaiah 7:9. Assent to a certain view of the nature of the subject matter (a view which may be corrected in particulars by the later experience with the text) cannot be withheld. If someone were to approach and interpret a text without the necessary prior understanding, his results—whatever they might be—would have no independent validity since they would not have been based on true understanding. They could always be called into question by one who by virtue of his assent "really understands," and who is not obliged to submit his understanding to any criteria generally acknowledged outside the realm of the faithful.

The revival of sacred hermeneutics, then, tends to support the notion that only the members of a particular religion, only those whose life and thought are shaped by a particular text or body of doctrine, are qualified to render a correct account of that religion or its literature. The outsider has no independent access, and therefore no recourse if he happens not to agree with the interpretation proffered from within. Like Bultmann's existential encounter, though on somewhat different grounds, this path to understanding resists any sort of extrinsic validation or challenge.

The hermeneutical situation shaped by this discussion is not one which would raise the hopes of anyone seriously interested in understanding religions or religious texts other than his own, or even in reflecting critically upon elements of his own tradition.

Consider the theologian who wishes to understand another religion, and not simply to explain it on the basis of his own theology, because he wants to enter into conversation with its adherents with some sensitivity to their thought and life. His aim might be ultimately evangelical; or he might be hoping to correct and improve his theological interpretation of the religion by a clearer grasp of its own self-understanding; or he could be interested in working together with its adherents on some matter of common practical concern. In any case he needs an understanding which will sustain him in close contact with them, enable him to anticipate their attitudes and responses with some success, and allow him to sense the way in which the elements of their religion cohere and interact. Let us say that it is part of his own theological standpoint that there is no least common denominator to his religion and the one he seeks to understand, nor any acceptable meta-religious framework to which both might be referred. Further, it is a tenet of his faith—unlike certain others—that a person may not give his allegiance to more than one religion at once. Do these

convictions, required by his own theological position, necessarily render him incapable of achieving the understanding he
seeks?

Or take the case of the scholar in the discipline usually
known now as the history of religions. Perhaps it is fortunate
that he often ignores the hermeneutical discussion—or dismisses
it as presumptuous speculation—and just goes about his business.
His response to what appears to him as a body of abstract, pre-
scriptive, and largely negative theory is understandable. But
it has some unfortunate consequences. One is the encouragement
of a tendency to emphasize the strictly critical and empirical
dimension of the discipline, implied by the word "history" in
its title, and to renounce, not only any evaluative interests,
but also any very great attention to the personal, intellectual
and affective dimension (one might say the "spiritual" dimension) of the religions studied. This concentration on the
"factual" is not always inconsistent with a second result of
the avoidance of hermeneutical reflection: the frequently implicit and sometimes unconscious acceptance of the hermeneutical assumptions of those nineteenth-century scholars who
provided the theoretical and material foundations for the modern historical study of religions.

Under these circumstances the historian of religions appears vulnerable to the believer's charge that he does not
"really understand" his religion, and that he is offering only
a reductionist account of it based on his own hidden premises.
The scholar may choose not to respond to such charges—particularly if he is confident of his procedure and doubts the
believer's competence to judge the adequacy of his treatment.
Or he may say that the limited scope of his treatment corresponds to a limited intention: he wanted only to explore a
certain aspect—say, the impact of a religious custom upon a
given institution—and does not pretend to have achieved or
communicated a full understanding of the religion.

But if such an understanding was indeed his goal, and he
wishes to meet and refute the charge of failure, he may explicate his hermeneutical principles and reveal the hypotheses
or convictions on which they rest: for example, a theory of
religion, a philosophical anthropology, or the positing of an
identity in "transcendental subjectivity." Such theoretical

props for a bridge to the object may not be any more convincing
to his religious critic than they are to Gadamer, especially if
they are in direct or implied opposition to the doctrines of
the religion itself. The "understanding" they sanction is then
unmasked as a rationalization based on the prejudices of an
alien culture or serving the interests of another religion.

If he takes this sort of objection seriously (and he must,
is he expects his own work to be taken seriously by an inter-
cultural and inter-religious community in his field), the historian of religions finds himself sharing the perplexity of the
theologian facing his own tradition, or the theologian confront-
ing another religion. All want to attain a valid understanding
of a religion and its literature, without relying for that
validity upon hypotheses which are theologically or religiously
unacceptable, and without surrendering their own religious
identity or critical freedom. And they want to challenge the
right of anyone to deny, summarily and without appeal, that
they might understand given these conditions. If the definition of understanding is to be at issue, they may ask, what *is*
understanding? When is a person justified in claiming it?
How can he know when he understands? How can his claim be
validated or defended?

Joachim Wach once remarked that the old hermeneutical
questions and problems have a way of recurring, and that later
inquirers often frame their questions and develop their solutions without suspecting that their way of going about it has
precedents.[17] That may be, of course, why the same issues
keep recurring. Wach's point may be less valid today than it
was when he made the observation, nearly fifty years ago.
More information concerning the history of hermeneutical theory
is readily accessible, at least; his own historical treatment
of the nineteenth century was a contribution of that sort.
Whether that history has been read carefully enough is another
question.

The first major figure in the tradition to which Wach
refers, Friedrich Schleiermacher, addressed his thoughts on
hermeneutics to what he regarded as a chaotic situation prevailing in the various disciplines and fields of interpretation.
Each seemed to have its own requirements for what would be

considered "understanding," and its own prerequisites and rules
of procedure for arriving at the meaning or meanings of a text.
There seemed to be no way to resolve the conflicting definitions and conflicting claims regarding understanding which
arose particularly where a given text was subject to differing
interpretative methods. The solution Schleiermacher proposed
was the development of a single, unified art of exposition,
based on "the simple fact of understanding," on the nature of
language and the basic conditions of the relation between
speaker and hearer.[18] Such a procedure, if it were fully developed and then applied strictly--that is, throughout the
expository process and not only when obvious difficulties arose
--would yield an understanding of definitive validity, elimi-
nating reductionistic and esoteric distortions. Dilthey
appealed to Schleiermacher's remarks to this effect in sketching his own view of the history of hermeneutics: The formulation of rules, and then of systems of rules, based upon the
practice of interpretative virtuosi, led in time to conflicts
among methods of interpretation. These disputes could only be
resolved by anchoring the correct procedure in an analysis of
the nature of understanding itself, and demonstrating the inconsistency of opposing methods with the requirements of the
process of understanding.[19] More recently, Gadamer's account
of understanding is similarly directed against a misuse of
the term. He counts himself part of the resistance against
the universal claims and pretensions of the scientific method,
and through his treatment of understanding he seeks to demonstrate that scientific investigation does not have exclusive
rights to truth.[20]

There seems to be a fundamental sympathy, on the part of
these hermeneuticians, with the situation of the theologian
and the historian of religions whose common problem was previously sketched: the problem is one of discovering a path to
valid understanding which does not depend, for its justification, upon theories or assumptions which violate the integrity of either subject or object, interpreter or text. Yet
the course of hermeneutical development, from Schleiermacher
to Gadamer and Betti, seems always ultimately to require the
introduction of theoretical commitments and of *a priori* conditions and limitations which tend to intensify the problem

rather than to bring it closer to resolution. It should come as no surprise if people prefer to get to work quietly at what Käsemann called the "practice of hearing," without stopping to consult the hermeneutical oracle beforehand. Nor is it insignificant that hermeneutics, in its post-Heideggerian phase, has tended to abdicate any responsibility for the guidance of interpretation in favor of concentration on its own intrinsic value as a mode of thought. When Betti protests against this recent development and appeals for a return to an object-directed hermeneutical enterprise, perhaps he errs--however legitimate his concern may be--in viewing the newer hermeneutics as a perversion rather than as an authentic fulfillment of some basic tendencies of the tradition.

In fact, if one goes in search of the "fundamentals" of the hermeneutical tradition, hoping to find the central core of assumptions or assertions characteristic of the leading figures as a group, their elusiveness may prove frustrating. A number of themes appear to run throughout the course of hermeneutical development, and it is tempting to try to draw some sort of consensus together. But few of these themes managed to survive intact for a hundred and fifty years. The possibility of understanding has been explained in terms of metaphysical principles, psychological similarities, and the relation of language to experience--to name three dominant approaches. But certainly no material agreement on these or on any other rationale has persisted from Schleiermacher to Gadamer. Schleiermacher found in the hermeneutical observations of F. W. Ast a doctrine of universal Spirit which served to eliminate the gap between subject and object in interpretation. It is clear that Schleiermacher's own philosophical position was congenial to this, although the degree of direct dependence of his hermeneutics upon philosophical support is difficult to assess, no matter how obvious the relationship may appear to someone who is looking for such dependence.[21] Dilthey was able to substitute a psychological for a metaphysical construct, in any case, while maintaining a continuity with Schleiermacher's hermeneutics; and Bultmann, still later, can discard both metaphysical and psychological theory, and base understanding upon the interpreter's life-relationship to the subject matter, and claim to be fundamentally consistent with the hermeneutical orientation of both Schleiermacher and Dilthey.[22]

A more durable consensus might be discerned regarding the problem of the nature of language and its relation to understanding. The idea that language (like all cultural products) is the expression of mind or spirit antedates Schleiermacher considerably, was shared by his pupil August Boeckh, strengthened under Hegelian influence, and developed by Wilhelm von Humboldt and Dilthey. It persists with further modifications in much later thought. This picture tends to encourage the notion that understanding is largely a matter of decoding language and of reconstructing the original spirit or psyche which comes to expression in a given work--a reconstruction which is possible because of the suprahistorical kinship of all individual minds and the consequent universality and timelessness of all "expressions." But again, the consensus on this point is not as stable as the persistence of this picture may lead us to expect. What Schleiermacher's own views are regarding the role of language in understanding is currently in dispute.[23] And the models of language as encoded spirit or experience, and of understanding as a reproductive process--influential as they have been--underwent great enough revisions during this century and a half to make any generalizations about their actual functions very tenuous and perhaps not very significant. Finally, Gadamer and his associates have repudiated any such model of understanding as the act of a subject who stands somehow outside language and uses the data of language as a means of access to the object. Language is not so much a bridge or a code between two independent minds as it is a medium embracing all "minds," and any understanding which is realized can only be in this medium and on its terms. With this development, where language itself is the active principle which initiates understanding, any continuity with the "expression" model of langauge would be difficult to find.[24]

The thread of continuity among the writers of the hermeneutical tradition, rather than consisting in any theoretical consensus of this sort, seems to lie in a common assumption, almost inherent in their language, which profoundly affects the way in which each of them states the basic problems. This is the assumption that "understanding" is the name of something. It denotes a mental process (a *geistige* or *seelische Vorgang*), a state of mind, an existential state--the terms will vary with other components of the hermeneutical structure. To clarify, nurture and sustain this state or process is the chief task of hermeneutics. It is therefore essential to determine the nature of understanding, and to investigate the conditions of its possibility. When Schleiermacher suggested that the truly definitive approach to hermeneutics would be to examine "the simple fact of understanding," he was inaugurating a partnership of hermeneutics and epistemology which was eventually to find a sort of culmination in the redefinition of hermeneutics by Heidegger.[25] Gerhard Ebeling emphasizes the unity of development from Schleiermacher through Dilthey to Heidegger, until "hermeneutics now takes the place of the classical epistemological theory" and becomes "the essence of philosophy."[26]

The major writers mentioned so far agree--if nowhere else--on the centrality of a determination of the nature and conditions of understanding to any adequate hermeneutics. Dilthey saw this demand as Schleiermacher's great achievement, and insisted himself that understanding was the name of the process by which one mind comes to know another (the *Inneres*, *Psychiches*) through the meaningfully given signs which are its expressions.[27] And Bultmann considers "the insight into the *process of understanding*, for which Schleiermacher once strove," to be the bulwark against superficial interpretations of texts.[28] Although he rejects Dilthey's "psychologism," Bultmann is just as firmly committed to the idea that understanding is a particular process or condition which can be analyzed and described. Gadamer, too, turns his attention to the foundations of the process of understanding, hoping, as he says, to "search out that which is common to all forms of understanding," and to indicate its general conditions, rather than being distracted to the consideration of particular problems of interpretation.[29] Perhaps Gadamer indicates the epistemological dimension most clearly, and at the same time points to a common source for his own statement of the problem and that of the hermeneutical tradition as a whole, when he says that his investigation "asks, to express it in Kantian fashion: How is understanding possible?"[30]

The attempt to structure hermeneutics in accord with a treatment of the problem thus stated has frequently given rise to new problems. Certain images of the nature of understanding which have been operative within hermeneutics have required, for example, the *a priori* determination of the nature of the object of understanding, or a particular normative relationship of reader to object (either demanded in the encounter of text and reader, or posited as pre-existent), or have required or implied a particular sort of anthropological or broader philosophical context. The raising of such theoretical (or, occasionally, existential) requirements within hermeneutics is problematical in the light of that concern for the integrity and freedom of both interpreter and text which has some place in the traditional hermeneutical enterprise. Further, a concentration upon the problem of the nature and transcendental conditions of understanding has often—either deliberately or inadvertently—left hermeneutics at some distance from the practice of interpretation.

The hermeneutical tradition has not taken a rigid channel, nor has the course of its development been inevitable. The internal criticism and debate which have contributed much to its growth continue, as recent discussion indicates. If the problems just mentioned were to be stated as criticisms of the tradition in general, they would be difficult to sustain against a recitation of specific countering examples. Yet it seems clear that the close association of hermeneutics with the transcendental inquiry into the nature of understanding, though generally accepted as necessary, tends to generate various difficulties and conflicts (if not always the same ones) within hermeneutics.

How might this situation be constructively addressed? The most promising approach, under these circumstances, would appear to be to undertake a close examination of the sources, conditions, and consequences of this association of hermeneutics with the theory of understanding within a specific hermeneutical account, in order to develop the elements of a constructive critique. That critique could then be carried out in such a way as to suggest concurrently a possible reformulation of the hermeneutical concern with the problem of understanding, pointing toward a resolution of some of the conflicts encountered.

Joachim Wach is a writer whose work might repay this sort of critical examination with particular regard to the problems involved in the interpretation of religious texts and discourse. Hermeneutical considerations in this field dominated his interests throughout his career. He sought consciously to be a representative of the "great tradition" to whose history he devoted considerable attention, and to work out the implications of that tradition for the field of religious studies. Both theology and the history of religions were addressed in his hermeneutical writings. Though his current influence upon the hermeneutical discussion in theology appears minimal (thanks in part to the Heideggerian turn which he, like Betti, regretted), his impact upon the history of religions is substantial, particularly through some of his American students. Wach's deliberate "representative" stance and his role in the explication of a hermeneutical position which has found fairly wide implicit acceptance in religious studies make his work valuable for the sort of inquiry we have in mind.

NOTES TO CHAPTER I

1. Rudolf Bultmann, "Is Exegesis Without Presuppositions Possible?", *Existence and Faith: Shorter Writings of Rudolf Bultmann*, selected, translated and introduced by Schubert M. Ogden (Cleveland: World Publishing Company, 1960), p. 294. See also Rudolf Bultmann, "The Problem of Hermeneutics," *Essays Philosophical and Theological*, tr. C. G. Greig (N.Y.: Macmillan Company, 1955), p. 241.

2. Bultmann, "Is Exegesis Without Presuppositions Possible?", p. 296.

3. Bultmann, "The Problem of Hermeneutics," pp. 255-256.

4. Hans-Georg Gadamer, *Wahrheit und Methode*, 2nd ed. (Tübingen: J. C. B. Mohr [Paul Siebeck], 1965), pp. xvi-xvii. Unless a translator is acknowledged, translations from foreign works cited are my own.

5. See Heinz Kimmerle, "Hermeneutische Theorie oder ontologische Hermeneutik," *Zeitschrift für Theologie und Kirche*, LIX (1962), pp. 120-123.

6. Ernst Käsemann, "Zum Thema der urchristlichen Apokalyptik," *Zeitschrift für Theologie und Kirche*, LIX (1962), pp. 258-259, as translated and quoted by James M. Robinson, "Hermeneutic Since Barth," *The New Hermeneutic*, New Frontiers in Theology, II, ed. James M. Robinson and John B. Cobb, Jr. (New York: Harper & Row, 1964), p. 43.

7. Emilio Betti, *Die Hermeneutik als allgemeine Methodik der Geisteswissenschaften*, Philosophie und Geschichte, 78/79 (Tübingen: J. C. B. Mohr [Paul Siebeck], 1962), pp. 30-31.

8. *Ibid.*, p. 7.

9. *Ibid.*, p. 29.

10. Fr. D. E. Schleiermacher, *Hermeneutik*, ed. Heinz Kimmerle, Abhandlungen der Heidelberger Akadamie der Wissenschaften, Philosophisch-historische Klasse, 1959:2 (Heidelberg: Carl Winter Universitätsverlag, 1959), p. 128.

11. Werner Schultz, "Die Grundlagen der Hermeneutik Schleiermachers, ihre Auswirkung und ihre Grenzen," *Zeitschrift für Theologie und Kirche*, L (1953), esp. pp. 159-168.

12. Wilhelm Dilthey, "Die Entstehung der Hermeneutik," *Gesammelte Schriften*, V, ed. Georg Misch (Leipzig: B. G. Teubner Verlag, 1924), pp. 329-330.

13. Kimmerle, "Hermeneutische Theorie oder ontologische Hermeneutik," p. 120.

14. Gadamer, *Wahrheit und Methode*, pp. xvii, 483-484; his response to Betti is quoted also in Betti, *Die Hermeneutik*, p. 51.

15. Carl E. Braaten, *History and Hermeneutics*, New Directions in Theology Today, ed. William Hordern, II (Philadelphia: Westminster Press, 1966), pp. 135-136.

16. Schultz, "Die Grundlagen der Hermeneutik Schleiermachers," pp. 159, 174-184.

17. Joachim Wach, *Das Verstehen: Grundzüge einer Geschichte der hermeneutischen Theorie im 19. Jahrhundert* (3 vols.; Tübingen: J. C. B. Mohr [Paul Siebeck], 1926-33), I, pp. v-vi.

18. Schleiermacher, *Hermeneutik*, p. 156.

19. Dilthey, "Die Entstehung der Hermeneutik," p. 320.

20. Gadamer, *Wahrheit und Methode*, pp. xxv-xxvi.

21. In the early "Aphorisms" on hermeneutics, Schleiermacher noted: "Alles vorauszusezende in der Hermeneutik ist nur Sprache und alles zu findende, wohin auch die anderen objectiven und subjectiven Voraussezungen gehören muss aus der Sprache gefunden werden" (*Hermeneutik*, p. 38).

22. Bultmann, "The Problem of Hermeneutics," p. 241.

23. For an overview, see Kimmerle's introduction to his edition of Schleiermacher's *Hermeneutik*, and the review of Kimmerle's position by Christoph Senft in "Die neue Aktualität Schleiermachers," *Philosophische Rundschau*, X (1962), pp. 288-290.

24. "To speak of understanding as an act, especially a productive or reproductive act of man, is essentially to misstate the hermeneutical situation at the very outset in the Heideggerian context, to fall in *Subjektivität*" (Richard Palmer, in the "Response and Discussion" following Gadamer's "The Problem of Language in Schleiermacher's Hermeneutic," *Schleiermacher as Contemporary*, Journal for Theology and the Church, VII, ed. Robert W. Funk [N.Y.: Herder and Herder, 1970], pp. 88).

25. For Heidegger, hermeneutics in its "philosophically primary" sense becomes an "analytic of the existentiality of existence," and hence the foundation for ontology. Martin Heidegger, *Being and Time*, tr. John Macquarrie and Edward Robinson (N.Y.: Harper & Row, 1962), pp. 61-62.

26. Gerhard Ebeling, "Word of God and Hermeneutics," *Word and Faith*, tr. James W. Leitch (Philadelphia: Fortress Press, 1963), p. 317.

27. Dilthey, "Die Entstehung der Hermeneutik," p. 318.

28. Bultmann, "The Problem of Hermeneutics," p. 237.

29. Gadamer, *Wahrheit und Methode*, p. xvii.

30. *Ibid.*, p. xv.

CHAPTER II

JOACHIM WACH AND THE HERMENEUTICAL TRADITION

The Context of Wach's Thought

When Joachim Wach was introducing himself to the audience
of his Barrows Lectures in India in 1952, he indicated to them
the three dominant interests of his career. The first was the
problem of understanding; the second, the sociology of religion;
and the third, the problem of the nature of religious experience.[1] These three are intimately related in his thought, and
it might be shown that his conception and disposition of the
first issue determined the course of his treatment of the
others.

Wach's concern with the problem of understanding was stimu-
lated by the situation in which he found himself when he began
his teaching at the University of Leipzig in 1924. He was the
first historian of religions ever to be appointed to the philosophical faculty there.[2] Apart from philological studies, the
study of religions had previously been carried on wholly within
the theological faculty. Wach had completed his own training
in the history of religions in the theological faculty two years
before, augmenting that program with work in philosophy and in
Oriental studies. Now he sought--with the support of his
teacher, Hans Haas, and in the face of several objections--to
introduce the new discipline of *allgemeine Religionswissenschaft*
into the liberal arts curriculum. In his inaugural dissertation, he presented a case for what he hoped to accomplish in
fact: the separation of *Religionswissenschaft*, in both its historical and its systematic dimensions, from the "normative"
disciplines, particularly from theology, and its recognition
and pursuit as an independent, "descriptive-understanding"
science.[3] Such a discipline must not begin by accepting a
normative predetermination of the nature of religion, or of
any particular religion, offered by the theologian or the
philosopher of religion. It must instead begin with the given,

empirical data of religion, and, by a method particularly suited
to its descriptive-understanding aims, attempt to confront and
interpret it.

Thus Wach began a lifelong concern with methodology. He
devoted considerable effort for the next several years to the
defense of the possibility of descriptive understanding, and
to the careful distinction of this approach from several other
kinds of treatment of religion. From Wach's standpoint, the
demand of certain theologians for a "normative understanding"
of religions--that is, for an interpretation of other religions
in the light of Christian revelation--is an arbitrary one,
leading to irresolvable conflicts among variant "understand-
ings."[4] But this demand is not the only threat to descriptive
understanding. Perhaps more dangerous is the allegedly objective explanation of the nature of religion advanced in the
name of psychology. In an early polemic against this treatment, Wach calls for a "critique of psychological knowledge"
to restrain psychologistic enthusiasm. The psychologizer, he
charges, knows no lovelier word than "only." "He is happy when
he has discovered that something is 'only' something." The
specific errors of this gleeful reductionism need to be clearly
indicated.[5]

At the conclusion of this attack, Wach mentions several
figures--Ranke, Boeckh, Burckhardt, Dilthey--as a modest selection of scholars who succeeded in discussing the human world
without falling into reductionism. They had a way of getting
to the heart of things, and of basing their observations upon
a comprehensive grasp of the object. We cannot simply imitate
them, Wach admits, but we should emulate them as models for
the understanding treatment of human concerns, including religion.[6]

This was not just a rhetorical nod to the good old days.
In fact, it was in the context of this search for an adequate
foundation for *Religionswissenschaft* that Wach undertook his
study of the history of nineteenth-century hermeneutics, which
issued in the three volumes of his *Das Verstehen* and in several
smaller publications. A broad range of interpretative theory
was considered in these works.[7] Certainly Wach believed this
study to be of more than antiquarian or inspirational value.
Like Emilio Betti, he perceived in the development of herme-

neutics from Schleiermacher to Dilthey the possibility of a
vindication of the ideal of objective, descriptive understanding. But while Betti's reliance on specific assumptions of
that hermeneutical development is largely unacknowledged, and
the long-range results of such reliance still unexamined, Wach
is prepared to develop both the assumptions and the lessons of
that heritage in some detail.[8]

Meanwhile, Wach initiated lectures at Leipzig in the sociology of religion, and published a brief introduction to the
subject in 1931.[9] The same methodological concerns are here
brought to bear upon another aspect of the study of religion.
After Wach left Leipzig (under Nazi pressure) and moved to
Brown University in 1935, he devoted more attention to sociology
and published another, more exhaustive treatment of the field
in 1944.[10]

Wach's sociology is hermeneutically oriented, and he saw
the development of an adequate sociology of religion as somehow
dependent upon the revitalization and expansion of the discipline
of hermeneutics. While much labor has been expended upon the
search for the correct approach to textual interpretation, Wach
felt, too little hermeneutical attention has been paid to the
sociological expressions of religion. Positivistic and func-
tionalistic sociologies are mistaken and misleading because
they do not begin with the recognition that the social aspect
of religion is the expression of a unique dimension of human
experience. Consequently they lack an interpretative method
which would do justice to the data. A unified hermeneutical
discipline would have to take into account the sociological and
practical, as well as the theoretical, expressions of religious
experience.[11]

The problem of the nature of religious experience itself--
the third area of Wach's concern--was one with which he did not
deal in any detail at first. It was not until he moved to the
University of Chicago, where he was chairman of the history of
religions field from 1945 until his death in 1955, that he
attempted to formulate an account of the nature of religious
experience.[12] Earlier, he had been reluctant to construct
such a theory; perhaps it would have been inappropriate in
view of his insistence on the freedom of *Religionswissenschaft*
from normative presuppositions, and its obligation to begin

with the given data and not with a theory of religion.[13] But
with the battle for the freedom of the discipline behind him,
and in a new cultural and theological situation, Wach turned
again in Chicago to the question of the relationship of the
history of religions to theology. He believed that the data
of his discipline could be useful to theology, and perhaps
especially to the theological understanding of other religions,
if a theory could be constructed from the data which might
serve as a "kind of *natural theology*" in the service of inter-
religious understanding.[14]

The relationship between Wach's theory of religion and
his hermeneutical position requires close examination. Whatever the circumstances of its eventual explicit development,
his account of the nature of religious experience may be taken
primarily as the unfolding of that prior notion of the nature
of religion which is required by his version of the hermeneutical circle, and which may be found throughout his discussions of religion.[15] The close relationship between Wach's
historical investigations in hermeneutics and his approach to
religious phenomena is evident.

Wach's indebtedness to those with similar concerns is
also obvious. His approach to the sociology of religion is
greatly dependent upon that of Ernst Troeltsch (with whom he
studied for a short time) and upon the "understanding sociology" of Max Weber.[16] In Wach's investigations of religious
experience, the influence of Max Scheler and Rudolf Otto is
visible and frequently acknowledged.[17] The greatest single
influence upon Wach's thought, however, was that of Wilhelm
Dilthey. His effect was most profound upon Wach's hermeneutical orientation (Wach dedicated the three volumes of *Das
Verstehen* to his mother, his father, and Wilhelm Dilthey),
but it pervades the entire range of his thinking. Wach viewed
the intellectual history of the nineteenth century through
Dilthey's eyes.[18] If he wrote scarcely at all specifically
upon Dilthey's work itself, perhaps it was because he found
little to criticize and, in fact, little to add.

Aside from these few, it is often difficult to judge the
extent to which any of the multitude of contemporaries and
predecessors cited by Wach actually had much impact upon the

direction of his thought. He has an appreciative word for nearly everyone, and he marshals support for his own observations
from quite divergent sources. At times--particularly in his
latest writing--this synoptic procedure creates a patchwork
effect which hinders the clear development of his thought, and
occasionally appears to commit Wach to conflicting or incon-
gruous positions.[19] He is certainly deliberate in his catho-
licity, however. Several of his students and colleagues have
commented upon his "irenic effort," his tolerant and gracious
disposition in scholarship as well as in personal life, which
he exercised not only in dealing with the plurality of religions
and cultures but also in assembling the material for his methodological reflection.[20]

Temperament is not the only factor determining Wach's attitude toward his sources. The impact of Dilthey's *Weltan-
schauungslehre* can be detected as early as Wach's first published work, his doctoral thesis at Leipzig.[21] There, and
again in his *Religionswissenschaft*, Wach recognized the potential usefulness of Dilthey's idea, that world-views and philosophies are to be understood as the products of different types
of psychic structure and different experiential patterns, in
the quest for the "intention" of religious expressions. He
called for a broader application of the doctrine than to strictly formal philosophical systems, upon which Dilthey and Jaspers
seem to have concentrated.[22] And here Wach followed his own
advice, not only by using Dilthey's suggestion in his approach
to religions, but also by trying to look beneath the outward
conflicts of various hermeneutical standpoints to find their
underlying concerns and to indicate their basic harmony whenever possible. Thus the coherence and common affirmations of
the entire hermeneutical development might be illuminated.
Wach draws upon divergent sources, not just to accumulate foot-
notes in support of his ideas, but because he wants to manifest
the unity which he believes often persists unnoticed in the
discussion. The result of this conviction is a treatment of
hermeneutical history which is selective, expository and appreciative, rather than strictly critical.

Rudolf Bultmann calls Wach's effort in *Das Verstehen* "an
extraordinarily careful stocktaking with a reserve which is in
my opinion far too great in regard to the position he himself

takes up--one which might illuminate history from the critical standpoint."[23] But Wach's historical study is not quite as lifeless and impersonal as this suggests. In it Wach is tracing the fortunes of the "great tradition" of hermeneutics from its inception in Schleiermacher's work to its eclipse by the growth of positivism in the final third of the nineteenth century.[24] (Dilthey's work remains outside his scope--as an object of inquiry; his presence in the book takes other forms.) He keeps his eye on several persistent problematic themes, discussing the way in which each of the masters of interpretative theory dealt with them. Gradually, it appears that certain hermeneutical constants might be indicated on the basis of the history of the problems. In occasional brief suggestions within *Das Verstehen*, and in several of his later articles, Wach presents a distillation of these constants. Thus abstracted from their context, the summaries are likely to appear simple and rather arbitrary, or (as Bultmann said of one such article) as "just the old hermeneutic rules."[25] Perhaps the abstraction is unfortunate; the context is essential to an appreciation of Wach's intent.

Then why did Wach choose this mode of presentation, this didactic style? It would seem to have been shaped by his own understanding of his role. Bultmann is not the only critic to complain of Wach's reserve, his reluctance to take up a definite position or to develop his own thought constructively.[26] But Wach did not see his task as that of a creative theorist. He indicated repeatedly the need for genuine, constructive hermeneutics in religious studies, and he hoped for a revitalization of interest in the discipline. But his own contribution to such a revival was to be the more modest one of transmitting the lessons of the hermeneutical heritage of the nineteenth century, and of keeping that heritage alive. He wanted to serve as the representative of an entire intellectual endeavor, and not simply as the advocate of a particular viewpoint within it. He maintained a representative stance consistently, from his early years at Leipzig--where he viewed it as a contribution to the renewal of humanistic scholarship-- onward throughout his American career.[27] Here he was even more sharply aware of his position as a representative of the entire German academic tradition in the humanities (*Geistes-*

wissenschaften), finding himself in a culture which seemed more concerned with results and practical technique, and inclined to be impatient with broader methodological inquiries. Wach believed his special function in this setting to be one of bridging the gap between the programmatic work of traditional hermeneutics and the practical interests of his students in the history of religions field.

Since Wach's death, the methodological aspect of the history of religions, at least within the American context, has suffered neglect.[28] The gap between theory and the actual investigation and interpretation of religious phenomena was not permanently bridged by Wach's contributions to the attempt. Certain of his hermeneutical principles have been taken by some as axiomatic, with much the same serenity and confidence in their fundamental self-evidence with which he himself extracted them from the tradition.[29] It was not long, however, before several of his students and colleagues began to express some uneasiness at the lack of constructive hermeneutical reflection. Several appeals have been issued for a creative attempt to overcome this deficiency.[30] Whether these appeals will encourage any reconsideration of the foundations of hermeneutics in the discipline is yet to be seen. Generally, the basic validity and adequacy of the approach represented by Wach has been assumed as a foundation for any future construction.[31] His hermeneutical work--and through it, the nineteenth-century tradition-- still has force.

Wach's Account of Hermeneutics

The history of hermeneutics in any given field, according to Wach, is always the history of the relationship of that field to philosophy.[32] This does not imply the existence of any firm and constant relationship between philosophy and hermeneutics. Hermeneutics is practically a primeval concern, antedating the establishment of any particular philosophical dependence. The need to reflect upon the nature, possibilities, forms and limits of understanding arose from the early recognition of its centrality in human existence--a recognition prompted by the experience of misunderstanding. The roots of theory are to be found in those situations in which normal, spontaneous, unreflective understanding failed, and incomprehension or error had to be deliberately overcome.[33]

Understanding is more likely to be a problem, and to be acknowledged as such, among those whose concern is with the proper interpretation of a text or a body of literature from the past. The legal, religious, and literary spheres, accordingly, are those within which hermeneutics has received the most concentrated attention.[34] Wach accepts and elaborates upon Dilthey's account of the rise of the discipline of hermeneutics in this context.[35] It was in the area of the interpretation of religious literature that the leading developments toward a discipline occurred. As in other fields, rules and practical helps for understanding had been gradually accumulated and transmitted, within the framework of a normative tradition of interpretation. With the Reformation, the situation changed: the authority of the tradition which gave sanction to these rules was challenged, and in its place the concept of the *perspicuitas* of Scripture--its immediate accessibility to understanding--was asserted. It was soon discovered that this liberation of the reading of Scripture from the *magisterium* meant in effect that the guidance of a unified tradition was replaced by a multiplicity of theories, doctrines, and procedures of interpretation, each claiming that true understanding lay in its direction alone. Not only were there vast discrepancies among the hermeneutical approaches of the various disciplines, as before; now conflicting treatments of the same body of literature were being advanced, with no apparent means of resolving the dispute. A state of conflict, the "chaos" to which Schleiermacher refers, persisted into the nineteenth century, when it was only partially subdued by the rise of a general science of interpretation.

It was in the post-Reformation struggles that the career of hermeneutics became closely bound up with that of philosophy, for the first attempts at a general theory of understanding were inspired by a philosophical vision: that of Spinoza, for instance, or of Leibniz and Wolff. A universally acceptable principle was sought, upon which both the possibility of understanding and a definitive description of its nature could be established. After the Kantian challenge to metaphysics, a philosophical interest in the foundations of understanding was kept alive by those who stood at some distance from Kant,

such as Hamann, and, especially, Herder. The stimulus of
Herder's thought upon hermeneutics at this juncture is particularly important from Wach's point of view.[36] Herder's ideas
on understanding were never systematically presented, but
lacked no impact on that account. Two themes in his thought,
when taken together, seem to stand out as hermeneutically significant: One is his insistence that the Bible is not a book
sui generis, but belongs rather to a particular class of literature, within the general realm of human expression, whose
function is the divine education of mankind toward the ideal
of "humanity." The second is the idea that understanding is
the very special agency through which man progressively rea-
lizes his humanity. Understanding drives beyond the husk, the
mere words, of a text, to discern--in what is essentially a
recognition--its inner spirit and source. Herder thus gave
impetus to further reflection upon the subjective, intuitive
dimension of the unique phenomenon of understanding, and at the
same time lent his support to the placing of theological within
religious hermeneutics, and religious within the context of
general hermeneutics.[37]

   Wach would be likely to concur in Dilthey's estimation of
Herder as having "come closer to true hermeneutics than anyone
else before Schleiermacher."[38] Wach stated simply, "One could
say that to the same extent as they exhibit Herder's influence,
the philosophers of the post-Kantian era showed a consideration
and appreciation for the problem of understanding."[39] The significance of that influence in the rise of modern hermeneutics,
and particularly in Schleiermacher's thought, has not been sufficiently recognized, according to Wach; perhaps it is because
it comes in so many forms and through so many different agents.
It came upon Schleiermacher through several mediators, including F. W. Ast and Friedrich Schlegel, as well as directly, and
is incorporated into his development of the first comprehensive
treatment of general hermeneutics.[40]

   Schleiermacher had no philosophically-inclined successor
in the field of hermeneutics. His students, including Boeckh,
lacked his interest in the theoretical foundation of a universally valid hermeneutical program, and turned instead to more
limited and concrete problems, mainly within philology. And
apart from his students, Schleiermacher had little immediate

impact upon Biblical hermeneutics. The grammatical-historical
method of J. A. Ernesti still ruled there, through such followers as Keil, Bretschneider, and Griesbach. Critics who were
united in their opposition to the sterility of this strictly
objective approach, objecting to its exclusion of any subjective element in interpretation, were divided when they tried to
offer constructive alternatives. There was no common agreement
as to what "understanding" might be or how it might be realized,
and appeal was made to a great variety of reference-points.

It was the work of Hegel, another recipient of Herder's
influence, which again aroused interest in the possibility of
a general philosophical account of understanding. But the distance of his thought from all concrete disciplines brought
about some extravagant simplifications of the issues by those
of his followers who tried to apply it in specific fields of
interpretation. Scholars in those fields often reacted strongly
against such mistreatment. Most later theorists who contributed at all to a general account of understanding were influenced by Hegel, but had to abandon him eventually (as did
Humboldt, for example) when they became aware of his lack of a
sense for historical particularity, for the rights of the concrete.[41] If they remained Idealists, at least their philosophy
was tempered by a growing respect for the individuality and the
special requirements of their subject matter. They tried to
steer a course between abstract reflection and empirical research. Their efforts were swept away, however, in the general
reaction against *Hegelei* in the last third of the nineteenth
century, when nearly any speculative or theoretical work came
under suspicion. The rise of positivism in most disciplines
created an almost total indifference to hermeneutics, and a
simple reliance upon empirical, philological study. This was
a departure even from the earlier grammatical-historical advocates, who had at least taken the trouble to clarify their
presuppositions and to offer some justification for them.[42]

Wach does not carry his account of hermeneutical history
explicitly beyond this point. The next significant development
from his point of view, however, was the work of Wilhelm
Dilthey, who took seriously both the inquiry into the foundations of understanding, as this had been pursued since
Schleiermacher, and the protests against speculation, as

developed classically in British empiricism and French positivism. "Dilthey," according to one of his expositors, "was
the first writer to set speculative questions aside and study
the process of sympathetic understanding soberly and scien-
tifically."[43] He wanted to revive the legitimate intention of
the hermeneutical tradition and to maintain and develop it as
an alternative to a thoroughgoing positivism. It was Wach's
aim to share in this effort, dealing especially with the contributions of the tradition to the problems of understanding
religion. Wach, like Dilthey, was convinced that the significance of Schleiermacher for the proper development of hermeneutics had not yet been truly recognized.[44]

Already in Schleiermacher's formulation of the problem,
Wach detects the presence and importance of two related themes,
whose course he then follows throughout the history he depicts.
The sensitivity any theorist demonstrates concerning these
themes, and the depth of his treatment of them, are a reliable
index to the potential adequacy of his hermeneutics. The
first is that of the portrayal and defense of an ideal of understanding which excludes all reductionism, extrinsic evaluation and pre-judgment, so that the object may be simply heard
and grasped as it truly is. The second is that of the proper
development, balance and interplay of the two principal aspects of the process of understanding: the empirical and the
a priori, the deductive and the inductive, the literal and the
spiritual. Achieving the correct harmony in the act of understanding is an art, as Schleiermacher observed; but the theory
of understanding can and must concern itself with the requi-
sites, the "preparation" of the interpreter in the broadest
sense, and go ahead to establish the basis for their relationship. No hermeneutics is adequate which does not come to
terms with this question.[45]

In his handling of each of these central themes, the
theorist reveals the nature of his dependence upon some ultimate frame of reference, and the question of the status of
hermeneutics itself and its relationship to philosophy on the
one hand, and to the subject matter of a specific field of
interpretation on the other, must be considered.

Wach's own response to this last question echoes Dilthey's

solution, insofar as he speaks of hermeneutics as the connecting link between philosophy and the individual human studies in which understanding is sought.[46] It has a certain autonomy from both, and represents the interests of neither exclusively. This freedom is evident in the dialectical development of hermeneutics, in which repeatedly an overemphasis on one of the two components of understanding just mentioned, the empirical or the *a priori*, would be succeeded by an antithetical stress on the other--a theoretical movement largely independent of both parallel developments in philosophy and of current exegetical practice in the disciplines concerned. Hermeneutics, Wach emphasizes, has its own spontaneity, a fact which should be pondered by those who would subsume it under philosophy as well as by those who would reduce it to a purely functional, practical dicipline. Either course would subject it to vicissitudes of growth of which it must remain independent if it is to carry out its own task.[47]

Further, though he does not develop the differences to any extent, Wach wants to insist that the hermeneutical approach to the question of the nature of understanding is to be distinguished from both the epistemological and the psychological modes of framing the issue.[48] Understanding "is not *just* a philosophical problem, although it is *also* that."[49] It is, on the other hand, a problem whose treatment must be responsive to the particular demands of a given field of understanding, as these have been revealed in exegetical history, but cannot be completely dominated by them. "It is our conviction," says Wach, "that the science of interpretation as a whole presents a most complicated, but therefore also most interesting *interweaving of experience and thought*, which must be·grasped and appraised from the side of the history of practice as well as from that of purely abstract, philosophical theory. Precisely then, but also only then, will we understand the unique and so eminently important mediating role of hermeneutics between philosophy and the human sciences."[50]

One consequence of the distance of hermeneutics from philosophy is that it is impossible to determine *a priori* what understanding will involve in any given area of inquiry; the course of the actual struggle to achieve an understanding of this particular material must be studied, and we must learn

from it, before we are in a position to discuss the nature of
understanding in any meaningful way.[51] But at the same time,
the distance of hermeneutics from the frame of reference of
each discipline means that the hermeneutical investigation may
result in a specification of "understanding" quite different
from that which the discipline itself is accustomed to require
or allow. Here, the hermeneutical theorist appeals to standards
or to general assumptions concerning the nature of understanding
which transcend the norms of the specific field. The classic
example is the dispute between the proponents of general and of
"sacred" hermeneutics in Biblical interpretation. The critics
of general hermeneutics charge that it is incapable of doing
justice to the text in its uniqueness, its absolute incompara-
bility to other literary works. An interpretation based on
general principles rather than on the particular norms and
assumptions of faithful understanding will inevitably miss the
heart of the subject matter. To this, the advocates of general
hermeneutics reply that all literary works exhibit a structural
similarity, by their very nature as products of the human mind,
which renders them accessible to an understanding proceeding
from general principles.[52] Further, an individual text may be
subsumed under a more definite class of works (e.g. "religious
documents") bound together by more qualities held in common,
and these qualities may be taken into account so that both the
nature of the text and the requirements of valid understanding
are respected. It is not the case, then, that alien standards
are being imposed upon the text.[53]

These claims of the general theorist about the nature of
the text are no more self-evidently true than his opponent's
contention that the text is finally unique and outside the
realm of ordinary understanding, although the cultural climate
of an age may favor one view over the other. The support he
offers for these claims is an integral part of the argument
the general theorist is obliged to put forward in defense of
his principal assertion: that certain basic requirements must
be met before any treatment of a text is entitled to the name
of "understanding." Other approaches to a text may be legitimate in their own way, for certain purposes; but "understanding"
designates one definite, particular phenomenon, and should not
be abused. Understanding is essentially the process--or

combination of process and act--in which a recognition of the
authentic meaning of an utterance is attained. It is the task
of hermeneutics to safeguard this process.[54] "Understanding"
must be defended, as Dilthey suggests, against those who deny
the possibility of such an achievement and against those who
appropriate the term falsely.[55] That defense requires a philosophically grounded (and hence generally valid) account of the
possibility, nature, and prerequisites of understanding.

The substance of hermeneutics, then, is the theory of understanding, comprising the two concerns which Wach traced as
themes throughout the history of modern hermeneutics: what understanding is, and what it presupposes, with regard to a given
area of interpretation. This theoretical presentation has
priority over any immediate practical utility in the interpretation of texts, although this is often expected of hermeneutics.
It has its own intrinsic value.[56] Here hermeneutics bears a resemblance to logic, one recognized early in hermeneutical reflection and mentioned more than once by Wach: It is a lament-
able fact that there is no certain correlation between a knowledge of logic and an ability to think logically.[57] "The great
interpreters are not always the great hermeneuticians as well,"
as Wach observed near the conclusion of his historical investigations.[58] Yet hermeneutics is not a formal branch of
philosophy (part of its distinction from logic, as Schleiermacher recognized[59]), and, whatever its distance from the actual
business of interpretation at any moment, it is always directed
toward the problem of understanding a given range of finite objects: the fixed expressions of the human mind. In this limi-
tation of the scope of hermeneutics, Wach again follows Dilthey
and manifests his opposition to Heidegger.[60] To speak, as
Heidegger does, of "hermeneutical phenomenology," of an "existential interpretation of existence," is misleading, when what
he is really proposing amounts to a metaphysical explanation
(*Deutung*). Hermeneutics is transformed thereby into philosophy
and loses its essential point of reference: an utterance, a
text. "We *understand* neither God, nor life, nor the world,
nor a man," Wach counters. "There is no 'exposition' [*Auslegung*] of existence, there are only attempts at an explanation
of it. . . . The limits of *finite* meaning are also the limits
of understanding; God, world, man--here there is no longer

finite sense. We never understand 'history,' but we do understand the utterances which lie before us as historical materi-
ial."[61]

The restriction of understanding to finite objects, and
further to fixed expressions or utterances of human beings, is
based on the requirements of understanding itself and not just
on a desire to keep things within tidy and manageable limits.
Like Schleiermacher and Dilthey, Wach does not believe that an
exhaustive account of the meaning (however "finite") of a text
can ever be extricated and set forth; and in that sense, understanding is always an endless process. And in any case, it is
not the purpose of interpretation to substitute a secondhand
analysis of the subject, a list of "results," for a living
encounter with the text. The practice of some interpreters
may give rise to the suspicion that hermeneutics sanctions
such treatment.[62] But the valid aim of interpretation, according to Wach, is to render the text comprehensible, to "awaken
understanding in others." Wach nowhere explicitly formulates
his own position concerning the relationship of understanding
to exposition, though it is an issue for many of the writers
he discusses. However, he does show great sympathy for
Schleiermacher's elimination of the *subtilitas explicandi* as
a separate category of concern within hermeneutics, and for
his recognition that the true aim (and best form) of "explication" is to induce the reader to share in the process of understanding itself.[63] Whatever information the interpreter
offers to the reader should not stand between reader and text,
blocking his access to it, but rather should be taken as an
aid in understanding, intended to lead the reader directly
into the text. The hermeneutical focus thus remains constantly
upon the nature of understanding. The greatest service of
hermeneutics, in the long run--and here Wach would affirm the
seminal observation of Schleiermacher--is to maintain this
focus.

Wach takes it to be one of the lessons of hermeneutical
history that there are degrees or levels of understanding.[64]
Some of the disputes over what constitutes valid understanding
might have been avoided if this differentiation had been re-
cognized--or rather, if it had been kept more constantly in
mind, for Wach finds it recognized already in the interpretative

principles of Schleiermacher's forerunner, F. A. Wolf. When
you approach a text, according to Wolf, you should ask yourself
for whom your interpretation is intended; and the answer should
have some bearing upon the way you proceed and the sort of results with which you will be satisfied.[65] Wach finds it note-
worthy that historians and philosophers of history, as well as
theologians and expositors of Scripture, have spent a great
deal of time in debate over the definition of the *Suffizienz*
of understanding. What must any valid understanding of a given
literature include? Differences have arisen and persisted concerning the role in understanding of judgment, evaluation, and
personal involvement and response.[66] Of course, not everything
that has been claimed as an indispensable part or sign of understanding can finally be admitted and reconciled into a com-
promise scheme. One task of hermeneutics is to separate the
intruders from the genuine ingredients. But an awareness of
the legitimacy, under certain circumstances, of different gra-
dations within the genuine might eliminate the grounds for some
recurrent controversy.

Wach's notion of degrees in understanding seems to rely on
a suggestion of Dilthey's to this effect. Dilthey writes:
"Understanding manifests various degrees. These are determined
primarily by interest [*Interesse*]. If the interest is narrow,
so is the understanding."[67] "Narrow" here indicates a limi-
tation, not necessarily a defect. Sometimes we are rightly
satisfied with a rather superficial, external understanding of
a phenomenon, for a limited practical interest. At other
times, motivated by a different concern, we may seek the most
profound and detailed understanding of the same phenomenon.
Both are understanding, though not of the same magnitude.
Applying the notion to our specific field, Wach writes that
"it is conceivable that we could do justice to a particular
religious thought or act without being able to grasp others
appearing in the same context or to grasp this context as a
whole."[68] The broader understanding requires, among other
things, a more complex and comprehensive interest.

Wach advocated a closer study and determination of the
sorts of "interest" which might have a legitimate role in understanding, and the contributions of each. While there can
be no understanding without some kind of interest or aim, some

interests may lead to uses of a text which subvert understanding completely, or which have a proper culmination outside it.[69]
(An instance of the latter is the practical interest of the
theologian, who wishes not only to understand his text but also
to appropriate its content for the life of faith.[70]) Wach was
generally more concerned with the demarcation of the realm of
understanding from other activities with regard to a text than
with making fine distinctions within that realm. He was content
simply to distinguish "partial" understanding--which presumably
includes different levels or dimensions--from that understanding
which is as near to perfection as human beings can attain:
"integral comprehension." This phrase recurs frequently in
Wach's writings to designate the *telos* of all understanding,
and particularly the ultimate goal of the interpretation of
religious texts--a goal whose integrity hermeneutics must maintain.[71]

Integral comprehension is not an absolutely accurate or
complete understanding. That remains an ideal, only approxi-
mated in practice. The integral comprehension of an utterance
is, however, "an all-inclusive interpretation of its significance."[72] Further elucidations of the phrase are rare, and
usually quite as vague; but in one place Wach offers a fuller
description, relating to the study of religious material:
"Interpretation of expressions of religious experience means
an integral understanding, that is, full linguistic, historical,
psychological, technological and sociological inquiry, in which
full justice is done to the intention of the expression and to
the context in which it occurs, and in which this expression
is related to the experience of which it testifies."[73] Such
comprehension demands all the resources of the interpreter:
not only his technical skill and knowledge, but the totality
of his character, his whole heart. (*Totalität des Gemüts*--
"totality of mind and soul," Wach renders it once. Dilthey
is the immediate source of this expression for him, though the
concept has a much longer history.[74]) The implications of
this total demand are significant, and require consideration.
So also do the terms in which Wach's description of "integral
comprehension" is framed.

Wach's appreciative and conciliatory approach to the past,
his desire to discover the unity in the tradition, may have

helped him progress toward the formulation of the harmonizing
concept of "integral understanding." But the major impetus to
the idea would appear to be his conviction that understanding
is in fact a unified process and must be treated as such. In
all its degrees and dimensions, understanding is distinguish-
able as something particular, something set apart from other
human activities, and internally consistent throughout its
operation. Hermeneutics is concerned with "what goes on within a person" when he enters into an understanding relationship
with an object.[75] The sudden catch or jump of insight ("I've
got it!") which is often the fulfillment of understanding, is
not the decisive point for hermeneutical study. It is of
psychological and epistemological interest, of course; but it
is the process which *leads* to that momentary act and which
makes it possible which is of primary concern from the standpoint of hermeneutics.[76] The existence of such a special process has been affirmed by modern hermeneutics ever since F. W.
Ast characterized it as the repetition of the creative process
itself.[77] Several modifications of Ast's thesis have been offered; but an adherence to some form of the notion that understanding is a process which permits a uniquely fitting apprehension of its object is a hallmark of the hermeneutical tradition.

What goes on within a person when he understands something?
Basically: a contact is made, a relationship is established,
between subject and object. Without this, the object is mute
and inaccessible, no matter how it is manipulated and analyzed.
Wach does not minimize the importance of objective study and
investigation: "There is no hope of understanding a religion
without the most extensive information possible."[78] But the
compilation and analysis of data can yield only a certain sum
of facts, variously arranged--not the unity of meaning (*Sinn-
einheit*) achieved in understanding. The contrast between understanding and the purely "scientific" treatment of material
was recognized by Ast, and has remained significant in later
development.[79] It was one factor in the opposition to the
strict grammatical-historical movement in theological hermeneutics. A failure to honor the distinction is partly responsible for the naiveté and sterility of positivistic treatments
of religious phenomena, in Wach's view.[80]

Understanding requires a blend of the empirical and the *a priori*, of what can be found in the text by objective means and what the interpreter must bring to the understanding relationship. The precise ingredients, and their proportions, and the proper way to blend them, have all been sources of contention. Just any sort of encounter with a text is not understanding, certainly; in dealing with any unfamiliar material, it is probably the rarest of relationships and is attained only through sensitive and deliberate effort. Our first reaction to an alien phenomenon, for example, is usually to try explain it so that it will fit in with our previous knowledge and convictions. We impose an interpretation or (more accurately) an explanation (*Deutung*) upon it, often singling out and magnifying one factor within it which can be harmonized with our previous position-- whether that position be a formal system or a less highly structured world-view.[81] Rationalistic and psychologistic explanations of religious phenomena are two of the more common instances of this response.[82] But it is not always the outsider or the critic who resorts to explanation as a substitute for understanding: the theologian who imposes normative presuppositions upon his text may find himself judged in the same company. The interpretation of the Bible, if it is to be an understanding, has no more right to be based on a special system which grants immunity from certain questions and risks than any other attempt to understand a text.[83] It was to distinguish understanding from forced explanation of any kind that the old hermeneutical maxim arose: *Sensus non est inferendus, sed efferendus.*[84]

Whatever its basis, "explanation" in this sense is an effort to take account of the object without risking the security of the present arrangement. The object must be reduced to familiar terms, not granted its own, and even "explained away." A recognition of the impossibility of reaching true understanding in this way has sometimes led to a reaction to the opposite extreme, at which the interpreter is to yield himself completely to the object, withholding nothing. An early form of this was the romanticist renunciation of self, aimed perhaps at a total metamorphosis into the personality of the author. The distance between subject and object is wholly eliminated--or at least denied. The impossibility of such a

transformation is sufficiently shown, Wach says, by the example
of those who attempt it. The results are ludicrous, if the attempt is genuinely serious; otherwise it is only a tasteless
affectation.[85] It abolishes the interpreter's critical freedom
to no good purpose, and gives grounds for the simple equation
of understanding with complete sympathy, agreement, or even
identity.[86] Understanding fares no better when we examine certain radical tendencies in recent interpretative theory, in
which decision and commitment are demanded as preconditions for
understanding and the goal of objectivity is regarded with suspicion as well as skepticism. "'Decision' is certainly--espe-
cially subjectively--important and indispensable," says Wach,
"but it relieves us in no way of the struggle to try to *understand*."[87] Judgment, decision, appropriation follow understanding, or at any rate they should follow it and not become confused with it. Of course the interpreter's own attitude toward
the object is always present, and develops along with his understanding; but its tendency to dominate and direct the understanding must be held in check by deliberate effort.[88] The
only "appropriation" which belongs to understanding itself is
the perception of whatever claim a text may make--but that
recognition does not mean assent.[89] All religious texts make
some sort of normative claim upon the reader, asking for existential appropriation. But only the Buddhist can accept the
claim of the Tripitaka, the Muslim that of the Koran. That
acceptance is not necessary in order to understand.[90] The interpreter must be able to withhold, or in any case to "bracket,"
his personal response, or he has surrendered the capacity for
objective understanding.

But does he have such a capacity at all? That seems to be
denied *de facto* by the allegedly objective interpretations of
religions by the non-religious, as well as in principle by
those who insist that understanding and appropriation are inseparable. The great historical studies of the nineteenth century have shown that our understanding is always conditioned by
all the factors which determine our situation: historical, cultural, geographical, sociological and psychological. These
cannot be erased; there is no "presuppositionless" understanding. Yet we can become conscious of our conditioning, and by
making allowance for it, achieve a "relative objectivity."[91]

Our conditioning is not allowed to dominate our approach to phenomena, as it is in the case of "explanation." Nor is it simply underlined as sufficient cause to despair of objectivity and to embrace some form of subjectivism. Instead, it is brought to consciousness by careful and discriminate effort, and its influence upon our understanding is then "neutralized" or "paralyzed."[92] The possibility of valid, unobstructed understanding is then open. "The principle of 'relative' (that is, the greatest possible) *objectivity* must be regulative for inquiry in the study of religions as it is for all inquiry in the human sciences," Wach writes.[93] It is a principle of great importance in his own hermeneutical theory.

Relative objectivity is possible because of that which is revealed when we begin to examine the various elements of our psychic constitution: the "relative *a priori*." Wach borrows this term from Georg Simmel and C. H. Steinthal to designate that which the creator and the interpreter of a work have in common, especially that which is universally human (belonging to the "*Ewigmenschliche*" or "*Mensch-Sein*"), but also more particular shared qualities.[94] Anything which can be understood belongs in some way to this "relative *a priori*"; it is an aspect of human being as such. It is this prior sharing which permits us, if we will, to penetrate to the authentic nature of that which seems alien, rather than seeing only the surface. We must grasp the "spirit" or the "intention" (the terminology varies throughout Wach's writings, with no apparent distinction) conveyed by a text, by neutralizing our subjectivity and allowing the *a priori* to come clearly to our consciousness. By that act we put ourselves within the hermeneutical circle, and can relate the "individual" to the "whole," the specific and unique aspects of the object to the spirit which gives it coherence.[95]

"Understanding is a recognition," says Wach.[96] He adopts Hegelian language, in one instance, to speak of it as a process in which the human spirit is impelled to recover a relationship to its "alienated" objectifications.[97] But Wach does not rely on the metaphysical identity of subject and object which the Hegelian terminology implies. Rather, with Dilthey, he speaks of the common characteristics of human minds (the "relative *a priori*," for Wach), which permit understanding to be mediated from one to another by means of the "objective mind" (*objektive Geist*)--the concrete expressions or objectifications of individual minds. Any human expression can be "re-cognized" or reclaimed by another mind, no matter how remote or strange the original expression may be to the actual life and experience of the interpreter. (Dilthey writes that, for example, he is able to understand Luther, even though Luther's form of religiousness is something he cannot admit as a possibility for his own life.[98]) It is not necessary to try to transpose oneself into the personality of an author, and to relive every detail of the procedure by which his work was conceived and created. That would be impossible in any case. We possess and can discover within ourselves all the resources necessary for recognizing and doing justice to the objective spirit as we find it in the text.[99] The basis for all understanding is thus self-knowledge: the discovery within ourselves of at least a latent form of that which we are to understand. "Only when I am entirely myself can I understand that which is foreign," Wach affirms.[100] And elsewhere: "The person who understands is distinguished by the ability to renew and revivify continuously his own experience as well as that of the race."[101] With such sentiments, Wach stands in continuity with a theme which owes its origins in hermeneutical thought to Herder: the idea that true understanding is the basic element in the "education" and development of humanity.[102]

The picture of understanding which Wach extracts from the tradition and presents to us through his own reflections obviously rests upon a foundation of more general principles concerning the conditions which make understanding possible and determine its operation. The closer we move toward a specific area of understanding (the interpretation of religious utterances, for example), the more often we are referred to other overarching principles relating that material to the phenomenon of understanding in general. This is inevitable, since Wach shares Dilthey's conviction that one cannot determine *a priori* what understanding will involve in any particular case.[103] The fundamental question whose answer requires an appeal to general principles might be expressed in this way: How can an object be "present" to or in the process of under-

standing which goes on within a person, making objective understanding possible? How can there be a correspondence between
object and understanding? And the question which arises in
connection with a specific field, requiring an appeal to more
specific principles, is this: What is it about this particular
sort of material (say, religious literature) which renders it
accessible to understanding? What is the object which is understood here? Combining the two lines of inquiry, then, hermeneutics for the study of religious literature must be developed in conjunction with transcendental principles which can
account for both the possibility of understanding in general
and the specific "comprehensibility" of religious texts.

The circularity which one senses in this assignment is
admittedly inescapable, and Wach rests within it agreeably
enough. One critic of his treatment of religious data observes
(with reproach) that "his 'objectivity' rests upon a philosophical choice."[104] Clearly Wach is implicated in the metaphysical bridge-building with which Heinz Kimmerle charges his
predecessors Schleiermacher and Dilthey.[105] Wach would probably acknowledge the accuracy of these charges, while questioning whether they amount to valid criticism. Wach did not regard philosophical commitments in hermeneutics as a handicap;
in this respect he was more free from the positivistic ethos
than was Dilthey, and less suspicious of speculative theory
than the existential phenomenologists.[106] In Wach's view, the
primordial phenomenon of understanding itself rests upon certain conditions in reality--in man and object. The theory of
understanding must simply acknowledge and attempt to explicate
that dependence. He states repeatedly that every account of
understanding must begin with an explicit or implicit "metaphysical decision," a "basic metaphysical conception."[107]
Whatever its advantages or disadvantages, it is there. The
kind of critical attention a theorist gives to it has a great
deal to do with the adequacy of his hermeneutics. The kind of
attention, not the amount, is crucial. If the philosophical
dependence remains unacknowledged or only vaguely recognized,
the theorist may be tempted by the illusory idea of "presuppositionless" understanding, instead of taking the trouble to
sort out the different varieties of presuppositions and making
discriminating decisions about them, in some sort of perspec-

tive.[108] Yet if the theorist chooses to dwell upon the philosophical aspect of his account, he may jeopardize the general
validity of his hermeneutics by constructing a philosophy of
understanding which is (strange as this may seem) too definite.
(Wach notes a certain correlation between definite and emphatic
philosophical convictions and hermeneutical fragmentation. The
proponents of general hermeneutics, however, are more likely to
err on the side of vagueness so far as metaphysical assertions
are concerned.[109])

Hermeneutics is not constructive philosophy; but it must
make some careful philosophical choices. Its best course, we
may gather from Wach's treatment, might be to define and adhere
to the philosophical essentials, the minimum with which it may
still be adequately supported. Here again--as with his account
of understanding as a whole--Wach does not develop his own position in any one place in an extended treatment, but gleans instruction from the history of hermeneutical theory. His conclusion seems to be that so long as certain minimum standards
are met, the philosophical options need not, and perhaps should
not, be foreclosed. A casual and diffident attitude toward
philosophy is preferable to a thorough commitment to a particular system in all detail. The latter may lead to a "dan-
gerously close connection between comprehension and explanation," as was the case with some hermeneuticians under Hegelian
influence.[110] In any case, it is likely to give occasion for
controversy and to limit the general appeal of the hermeneutical structure in the long run. Wach's own eventual philosophical choice was "emergent evolution," as developed by
Alexander, Lloyd Morgan, Whitehead, and especially William
Temple. Like the monism of some of Schleiermacher's fore-
runners and later Idealism, this philosophy relates the possibility of understanding to the participation of subject and
object in a common ground of being; but it surpasses these
earlier philosophies, according to Wach, in its ability to
give close attention to the "realm of the personal" and to
individual differences.[111] Wach does not go into any detail
concerning the relative advantages of his choice, and it is
evident that he regards it (from the hermeneutical standpoint,
at least) as no more than a preference, surely not a requirement. The relativity of all philosophical systems was a lesson

he learned from Dilthey and took to heart when he sought a basis for hermeneutics.

The minimum standards for such a basis are set by the two sorts of fundamental questions, mentioned above, which necessitate an appeal to transcendental principles: the possibility of objective understanding in general, and the "comprehensibility" of the specific material to be studied (for Wach, religious writings) must both be established. The most cautious attempt to meet these standards with the least possible involvement in "speculation" was probably that of Wilhelm Dilthey, and Wach takes his bearings, again, from Dilthey's effort. Dilthey hoped to base a satisfactory account of understanding upon a strictly empirical investigation of mental life, a "descriptive-analytic" psychology. The investigation was to yield two principles which are hermeneutically significant. As H. A. Hodges states them, they are "first, that human nature is everywhere the same, i.e. that the elementary components of mental life are common to all men, and second, that every expression is constantly connected according to a rule with one such common element."[112] These principles are reflected in Wach's use of the term "relative a priori," that common fund of the eternally human by virtue of which we may discover within ourselves the enlivening "spirit" of any human utterance.

According to Hodges, Dilthey was aware of a conflict between his desire for an exclusively empirical psychology and his need for universally valid principles of mental life. Such principles as the two just cited could only be hypothetical. After the development of clinical psychology, Dilthey acknowledged the difference between a strictly descriptive method and what he came to call his "structure-psychology" or "anthropology," which then assumed a more explicitly normative theoretical role in his later writing.[113] Wach does not regard Dilthey as an exception to the rule that every hermeneutical effort begins with a metaphysical decision; and Dilthey's own recognition of his situation is testimony in Wach's favor.

In the methodological section of his comparison of two concepts of salvation (his first published work), Wach sketches a philosophical psychology or anthropology somewhat after Dilthey's model, indicating some of the basic components of personality.[114] Anthropological theory never assumed a central

place in his hermeneutical thought, however, although it was
occasionally brought in on the periphery. Psychology and anthropology may lend their support to the principles upon which
hermeneutical theory of understanding is based, and their contribution is not overlooked. Wach writes, for instance, that
"Eduard Spranger in his illustrative investigation of the primary levels of reality consciousness . . . has proven that in
all of us there are latently present certain more primeval
structures of consciousness. What is called 'mind' has the
ability to activate these and to understand, so to speak, the
atavistic and distant expressions of our soul, the expressions
which are alien to our present consciousness."[115] Such confirmation, however, is not essential, and hermeneutics properly
maintains a distance from the concrete disputes and problems
of these inquiries.[116] Again, as in the case of speculative
philosophy, Wach is wary of any great preoccupation with philosophical anthropology, and particularly with the existential-
ists' "self-analysis." It tends to the same result: a dis-
traction from the material to be understood, and a consequent
inclination to explain rather than to understand.[117]

Wach is just as likely, therefore, to cite classical or
poetic expressions of the hermeneutical principles he wishes
to illustrate, as to seek more rigorous confirmation. They
are at least as valuable, as explications of the underlying
ground of understanding, as any modern scientific confirmation
or philosophical rationale. Novalis ("How can a man understand
anything, if he does not carry the germ of it within himself?"), Jean Paul ("In each man swell all the forms of humanity"), Goethe, and the Platonic principle of the correspondence
of the *logos* in things to the *logos* in us, are all invoked as
witnesses to the fundamental principle upon which hermeneutics
--and understanding itself--must ultimately depend.[118] The
most common embodiment of this principle in hermeneutical
theory since Ast has been the idea of the identity of human
nature; although this idea itself has been imbedded in various
contexts, it continually reappears as the "guarantee" for the
possibility of understanding and for the accessibility of any
human utterance.[119] In one form or another, Wach believes,
this idea is indispensable to hermeneutics.

Of course, the idea itself requires some further unfolding.

How is "human nature" identical? And how does this insure the comprehensibility of a given form of material? Here, too, Wach limits his remarks to general observations, seeking a broad consensus and avoiding any specific philosophical commitments. He favors what he calls a "spiritual" concept of existence, involving the recognition that each "empiric personality" is only a particular and partial actualization of a much greater field of potentials, common to all human life.[120] As Dilthey observed, the differences between individuals are never qualitative, but only variations in the degree to which each person has realized different aspects of the universal fund of possibilities.[121] Even when only latent, these possibilities are within the grasp of anyone and can be awakened, with more or less effort, under appropriate circumstances. They belong to the primordial structure of personal existence, which is everywhere and always the same. Wach finds confirmation of this insight in Jung's idea of the collective unconscious, as well as in Spranger's work.[122]

"Not everything is understandable in principle; but only that in whose nature I somehow have a part," writes Wach.[123] Sometimes we may expand our awareness of others, to enable understanding, by recalling our own past experiences--times or events in which we were perhaps more familiar with aspects of our nature which are now lost to consciousness. Remembering our childhood mentality, our games and associations, may give us insight, Wach says, into the "primitive mind," for the patterns of thought which dominate our childhood are "immersions into archaic modes of consciousness."[124] Memory allows us to explore our previous experiences and their roots as resources for present understanding. Certain memories and their psychic motifs may be repressed, of course, and therefore inaccessible in this way. An entire culture may also repress certain aspects of consciousness, making it difficult or impossible for its members to recover them individually and thus to understand other cultures where these aspects play a positive role.[125]

Fortunately we are not obliged to actualize every human possibility in lived experience before we are able to understand those expressions which arise from it. The same theorist who stressed the importance of experience, and urged the cultivation of a wide range of experience, as a preparation for understanding--Wilhelm von Humboldt--also strongly defended the important role of imagination (*Phantasie*) as its complement. Dilthey, Simmel, and Spranger have built upon his work.[126] A person's potential for experience is not exhausted with his external experience of life (*äusseren Lebenserfahrung*), Wach affirms. There is also "inner experience" (*inneres Erleben*) in which external experiences can be "anticipated," so to speak, and the bounds of the empiric personality widened in imagination far beyond the possibilities one human being could even realize in actual life. Contact with another person or culture through its expressions awakens the possibilities which lie dormant in the soul, and understanding is inaugurated.[127]

The natural disposition toward "substitutive experience" must be cultivated by the disciplined interpreter. He must be conscious of that element of human nature which gives rise to, and is addressed by, the forms of expression with which he is concerned. He must discover and develop his sense (*Sinn, Organ*) for the object with which he deals: the ability to recognize its place as a unique and irreducible dimension of existence. Such an acknowledgement and careful nurture of the "affinity," "spiritual kinship," "congeniality" which binds one's own life to the object reveals, finally, the true interest, the *inter esse*, which permits integral understanding.[128] The contrast between Freud's treatment of religion and that of Dilthey, one may gather from Wach's remarks, can be traced to the fact that Dilthey possessed a sense for religion, acknowledging its firm basis in the deepest grounds of personal existence, while Freud, by his own admission, lacked any such sense. Dilthey thus opposed any attempt to explain religion away, while Freud's insensitivity permitted him to construct just such a reductionistic hypothesis.[129] Wach finds it somewhat puzzling that Freud did not consider his lack of religious *Sensorium* a handicap which might impair the validity of his observations on the subject. It was a most serious deficiency, one for which no amount of external knowledge "about" religion can compensate.

What does a "sense for religion" involve? It is a consciousness of man's natural, universal disposition or *nisus* for religious experience. For Wach, religious experience is "constitutive of the nature of man."[130] It is a sort of

"structural *a priori*," an element--perhaps the chief element--
of the eternally human.[131] All those forms, institutions and
expressions which we recognize as "religious" may be referred
to this single, unitary phenomenon.

Religious experience is for Wach essentially an apprehension of "the numinous." Wach finds little to dispute in Rudolf
Otto's account of the experience of the Holy, though the specific distinctions and issues which Otto raises in his discussion
play little part in Wach's treatment of the experience.[132]
"The essence of religious experience--and in this it is distinguished from every other kind of experience--is the awareness of a supreme absolute power which we call God," Wach
declares.[133] It is "the most intense experience of which man
is capable," a total response to that which is apprehended as
"ultimate reality," compelling man to some sort of action in
response.[134] The universal capacity for this kind of experience is realized in the multitude of outwardly differing religions, with their doctrines, rites, and organizations.

All religions, then, have their origins in this single
human dimension, the "religious experience" or "universal religious consciousness." The primal intuition (*Ur-intuition*,
vision, revelation, experience of the Holy--all are nearly
equivalent terms for Wach) of the founder of a religion, mediated through his individuality and transmitted by his followers,
gives to a religion its characteristic "attitude." Jesus,
Mohammed, the Buddha, Laotse, and Zoroaster all had these pow-
erful intuitions.[135] In those religions where no historical
founder can be named, there is nonetheless a characteristic
experience of the holy which is determinative for its "attitude."[136] Wach believes that "if we can only pierce deeply
enough through the coating of customs and ideas which are
really only outward manifestations and lay bare the basic attitude conceived and nurtured by a decisive religious experience, then the various factors of religious expression will
become immediately intelligible, and seemingly divergent and
incongruent thoughts and acts will be found to contain one
central motivation."[137]

The connection between experience and expression should
be more closely examined. Each apprehension of ultimate reality already contains a "germ of theory," a range of possibilities

for its intellectual expression.[138] This relatively pure
essence Wach sometimes calls the "idea" of the religion. But
the experience drives toward more concrete expression: the
"idea" must be embodied in "concept" (*Begriff*) as an objectification of the human mind. As such it enters history, has
effects upon and is affected by its environment. The possibilities of the "idea" are immediately diminished by the finite
material to which it must subject itself in order to gain expression. All thought and expression alike is inadequate and
confining to an intuition of ultimate reality, and there are
particular additional limitations imposed by the specific intellectual and cultural situation which determines the available forms of expression. In the consequent and continual process of selecting and actualizing possibilities, the basic attitude or spirit of each religion manifests itself.[139]

The differences among the major religions can be attrib-
uted therefore to the varying resources and requirements of the
historical situations in which each of them developed its self-
interpretation and attitude. Differences in the temperament
and character of the founders—or of natural groups—also influence the way in which the basic religious experience is
apprehended, and affect the content of its theoretical minimum
or "idea" as well as of its more concrete manifestations.
Personal differences are at least contributing factors to the
heterogeneity of religious experiences; Wach confesses an inability to account for the obvious variety in any other way.[140]
Of one thing he is certain: all religious objectifications—
texts, institutions, art, ceremonies—are rooted together in
that aspect of the human *a priori* which he terms "religious
experience." Their comprehensibility is thus assured. They
are present to the process of understanding because they are
present in essence, in their irreducible significance, already
within the one who understands. Wach's objections to the attempts of Freud and others to explain religion by reducing it
to its empirical, historical, or psychological origins have
been mentioned. "Transcendental" origins are apparently a
different matter—and this difference is highly important—
for here Wach equates understanding the ultimate meaning of a
religious utterance or phenomenon with recognizing its inner
origin. "The ultimate source and meaning of an expression or

form valid in the realm of religion is its origin from, and testimony to, a significant religious experience."[141] "Source" or "origin" and "meaning" are equivalent. For Wach, this is not an arbitrary assignment of meaning, as if it were to put religious phenomena in their place within the framework of some hypothesis or world-view. This is the true nature and meaning of religion; we know, we recognize, we understand it to be so.[142]

As Wach understood it, the task of hermeneutics is to give an account of the nature of the process of understanding and to indicate the conditions which permit understanding to be realized within a given field of human expression. The first part of this task Wach addressed by delimiting understanding from some other activities with which it is often confused or conflated, and by sketching, in as broad and representative a fashion as possible, the authentic nature and the roots of understanding. The second part, the question of the conditions of understanding, concerns that balance of the empirical and the *a priori*, of objective textual study and the interpreter's preparation, to which any mature hermeneutical position must speak. Here, too, Wach wanted to pare away the inessential and the obstructive, particularly on the side of the *a priori* requirements. He wished to concentrate attention on the most direct route to integral comprehension.

Wach acknowledged the importance of the empirical or objective dimension of understanding, although he did little to develop the procedures involved or to specify the results this aspect of interpretation is expected to provide. In *Das Verstehen*, each new development in the history of objective interpretation is seen as a positive advance, so long as it is not prized as the sole and sufficient key to understanding. The accumulation and refinement of methods of objective study is welcomed. This dimension should include what Wach calls "a comprehensive description of the facts" (based chiefly on grammatical and philological analysis of the text in question), and "a historical and sociological explanation" of the content of the work.[143]

The other dimension--subjective, *a priori*, or "psychological"--is dominated by, and practically restricted to, the "sense for religion." Understanding may not proceed from a theoretical standpoint which somehow predetermines the nature and "place" of religion. The normative disciplines of philosophy and theology have no right to impose any preconception upon the work of objective understanding. But neither may one be derived from descriptive historical study, as a sort of intrinsic model. (Here Wach separated himself from Dilthey, suggesting that Dilthey's perplexity about the "circle" which seems inevitable in understanding religion stemmed from his desire to limit himself to historical method at this point.[144]) Understanding must begin rather from a "foreknowledge" (*Vorwissen*) or "prior insight" into the nature of the object, which the sense for religion grants the interpreter. It is this inner capacity, preceding all reflection and theorizing, and not some contrived "pre-understanding," which puts us inside the hermeneutical circle and guides our understanding constantly. We may, of course, express that prior insight in the form of a very general tentative hypothetical concept of the object, but its function and status is quite different from that of a normative extrinsic preconception which would prevent understanding.[145] (Wach's own depiction of the nature of religious experience may be taken as such a hypothesis, explicating the "universal religious consciousness." He once wrote that "our understanding of the nature of religious experience and its forms of expression is not an act of faith but a result of empirical observation and investigation," in that it is derived from universally available data. It is rooted in the pre-reflective natural insight of man, universally corroborated and independent of any particular standpoint.[146]) This true *a priori*, the sense for religion, must be the immediate source of whatever pre-understanding the interpreter brings to the text.

In order to understand a religious text, then, an interpreter must possess the most extensive information possible relating to the text; he must bring to it a cultivated sensitivity to the realm of experience which is expressed in the text (that is, a sense for religion); he must be able to exclude prejudice and to "neutralize" his subjectivity while engaged in interpretation; and his full interest must be directed toward the goal of integral comprehension. These are the conditions of

understanding.[147] The resulting blend and interplay of inductive and deductive elements in the understanding of any particular text is an art demanding flexibility and responsiveness
rather than an adherence to rules. The process culminates
ideally in a moment of sudden insight, when things fall into
place and integral comprehension is reached.[148] Although hermeneutics does not lend any practical assistance at this point
--not only the reflective character of hermeneutics, but the
artful character of interpretation, preclude it--the hermeneutical preoccupation with the questions of the nature and conditions of understanding here finds its fulfillment.

Hermeneutics and Practice

According to Wach, the understanding of religious documents is "only a special example of our capacity to understand
religious personality in general."[149] Without a prior sense
for the religious element in human nature, its written expressions would have no sense for us. The meaning of any religious
expression, as Wach puts it, is its origin in and witness to
religious experience. At the same time, the expression is indispensable for an understanding of the religious experience
of any particular person. "The religious experience of another
person can never become the object of direct observation,"
Wach states.[150] His experience exists for us only insofar as
it is expressed. We may have a prior grasp of the essence of
religious experience; but each expression, like each personality, has its own character or spirit, its individuality,
which cannot be simply subsumed under that which is "already
understood" in general, nor dismissed as an insignificant remainder. It is this particularity, neither common nor alien,
which we must seek to understand in each religious document;
the field of interpretation (remembering Schleiermacher) is
that which is understandable but not yet understood.[151] If we
were not interested in the particular forms which religious
experience and its expression have taken throughout history,
there would be no point to studying texts at all.

Our sense for religion gives us a preliminary grasp of a
text's content. Understanding begins, as Schleiermacher said,
in an act of "divinatory boldness," when this original pre-
monition is asserted.[152] But then how does it proceed? Each

text presents itself as a unique combination of elements. The
"idea" has clothed itself with whatever objective material was
available, so that the expression of experience has become en-
tangled with external objects and circumstances. The result
is a document whose authentic meaning is not perspicuous. "Externally religious documents form a part of a completed system
of thought, internally they are products of individuals' minds
and become again the reflections of individual experience,"
Wach writes. "The line between what happened within and what
happened without is not always easy to draw, and the interplay
of fact and fancy raises one of the most intricate problems in
correct interpretation."[153] Careful objective study may settle
some of the issues, but ambiguities nearly always remain. It
is impossible to determine by objective study alone just where
the "spirit," the living center, of a text may be. The dominant aspects may not be the most evidently dominant, and the
heart of the text may go almost unnoticed.[154]

As an aid to interpretation, Wach calls repeatedly for the
development of a "logic of the forms of religious expression,"
a "theory of religious language," a sort of "religious grammar."[155] The possibility of such a grammar rests upon the
great similarity which is evident in the structure of religious
expression everywhere. Religious experience tends naturally,
even necessarily, toward expression. Further, it tends to
manifest the same sorts of expression universally, and these
can be understood by anyone with a sense for religion--barring
other obstacles. The purpose of a religious grammar would be
to clarify and classify the various kinds of expression and
their corresponding varieties of experience, so that they might
be recognized as such regardless of their context or particular accidents of formulation.[156] At one time Wach suggested
the construction of a general theory of expression to advance
understanding in all the human studies.[157] He hoped that it
would be possible to match particular types of expression
with the "inner states" which produce them, and even to specify
the depth and authenticity of the experience with which any
expression is connected in a given instance.[158] This project
may have been closer to psychology than to hermeneutics in
his scheme of the disciplines; at any rate he gave it little
attention in his later writings. He chose to concentrate

instead on the problem of arranging and of classifying the forms
of religious expression. Part of the task here is simply to
furnish a taxonomy of the forms or structures of religious expression. Wach puts forward, without offering any particular
justification, some major categories for such a taxonomy (fur-
nished "*ex abrupto*," as a critic remarks[159]): Religious expression takes three forms, the theoretical, the practical, and
the sociological; its theoretical form may be impelled by three
motivations, the demonstrative or expressive, the communicative,
and the missionary, and it may have two modes, the endeictic
(symbolic, indirect, usually visual) and the discursive (explicit, direct, usually linguistic and audible).[160] Further,
the content of the theoretical or intellectual form of expression manifests three mains concerns: theological, cosmological,
and anthropological.[161] These may each be treated in mythical,
doctrinal, or philosophical terms, as well as symbolically.[162]

More than a list of categories is needed in dealing with
the content of theoretical expression, however, if an understanding of a specific utterance or text is to be attained.
Here Wach appeals to the concept of type. The close connection
has been seen: Herder derived the concept of type from his
studies of Plato, and it was thus introduced into modern hermeneutics. Humboldt was the first to apply it systematically,
and Dilthey gave it further attention, but its potential has
not been exhausted.[163] Typology not only arranges data in
meaningful patterns, as any form of classification might; it
also mediates between "empiricism" and "apriorism" in interpretation. The type is the point of convergence of the empirical and the *a priori* elements in understanding.[164] Among
the recurring themes in religious expression--prayer, sacri-
fice, enlightenment, grace, and so on--certain individual treatments may be taken as illustrative of the basic intention of
the entire theme: they may be called "typical," and allowed
to represent the type. They are more than illustrative examples, possessing the required assortment of characteristics;
they are "exemplars."[165]

The danger of typology in some of its forms (e.g. in
Weber's usage) is that it erodes one's sensitivity to historical individuality. Each phenomenon becomes just another speci-
men of a type. But if developed and used correctly, typology

should instead heighten our awareness of the particular by
allowing us to grasp its true character more readily. The type
can do this only if it is grounded in life and lived experience,
and not simply in a conceptual framework.[166] Its origin in life
preserves its flexibility and spontaneity. The truly typical
and exemplary--the "classical," as Wach came to call it--is
grasped as such intuitively. It strikes us as the most perfect
representative imaginable for a particular kind of religious
objectification.[167] Typology thus helps us to relate the
"facts" of the text to our *a priori* sense for its ultimate meaning as a religious expression, and thereby to discover the spirit and dominant traits of the text. It is not indispensable:
understanding occurred long before typologies might be constructed, even in difficult areas of interpretation. But typology can direct our understanding, narrow the potential range
of meaning, and spare us a great deal of effort as we seek that
element of the "relative *a priori*" to which the data may be related. Some acquaintance with typology, as well as with other
schemes of classification, therefore deserves a place in the
interpreter's preparation.[168]

The activity of understanding a text, as Wach presents it,
might comprise the following stages: First, the basic nature of
the text as religious expression is sensed in an initial intuitive divinatory presentiment or insight (*Ahndung*, to borrow
Schleiermacher's term). Next, the empirical study of the text
and context distinguishes the "inner" from the "outer" influ-
ences upon its style and content, and reveals those forms of
religious expression which enable us to identify patterns of
thought and to become familiar with the "grammar" of the text.
When these patterns are further studied, we come to recognize
one or more typical elements in the text around which the whole
seems to cohere. This is a second "intuitive" moment, requiring
an openness to "substitutive experience" and some familiarity
(which may or may not take the form of a typology) with major
forms of religious apprehension and expression. The grasp of
these dominant typical characteristics gives us the "spirit"
of the text. Then, finally, we may fill in the details by
relating specific facts to the dominant traits and vice versa,
in the familiar reciprocal movement between part and whole,
individual and general. The process is never complete, and

certain elements of the text may forever elude us. But if we
proceed in this way, we may hope to attain an accurate and
comprehensive understanding which approaches "integral comprehension."

Wach's interest in hermeneutics left him little time for
constructive work in the interpretation of religious texts. He
did not keep himself aloof from such work; he was obviously
well-informed on the history and current development of research
in particular areas.[169] However, his few personal ventures into
the practice of interpretation tend to take the form of methodological exercises and illustrations rather than of constructive material contributions to the understanding of the text.
Even his methodological suggestions, sketched above, are nowhere developed in any detail. Interpretation itself is over-
shadowed by his theoretical concern with the problem of the
possibility of interpretation.

It might not be justifiable therefore to take one of
Wach's interpretative treatments, his early treatise on the
Saddharma-Pundarika Sutra (the "Lotus Sutra," significant in
Mahayana Buddhism) as either the best possible interpretation
of which he was capable, or his definitive statement on that
particular text. It was written early in his career (1925),
and, even though it is his only publication of any length on
any text, it occupies under sixty pages. Nevertheless, it may
give us some idea of the consequences for the practice of interpretation of Wach's hermeneutical position. The adequacy
and technical accuracy of the treatment from the point of view
of contemporary Mahayana scholarship will remain outside the
scope of this inquiry, though such questions are far from irrelevant to any full evaluation of Wach's work.

Wach goes to the Lotus Sutra in search of the "religiosity"
of Mahayana Buddhism--that is, its "spirit" insofar as this is
determined by its religious orientation. (A "spirit" can also
be detected in the ethical and philosophical aspects of a religion, which are related to the anthropological and cosmological religious themes; but it is the theological which is
of central importance to the religion as such, and therefore
also to Wach's inquiry.[170]) Mahayana studies, he observes,
have been predominately historical in character. These should

be supplemented with an account of the nature of Mahayana as it is (in its "*Sosein*"): it is an original, highly individual phenomenon, which cannot be fairly treated merely by summing up its historical components or viewing it as a corrupt variant from earlier, purer Buddhism. It has its own new center, derived from the religious experience of certain disciples and followers of the Buddha--an experience which was different, from the very beginning, from that of those who founded the Theravadin schools.[171]

The Mahayana sutras are the repository for this characteristic religiosity: it is expressed in them, and they sustain it, in turn, in the adherents of the religion.[172] Here we may discover the "inner possibility" of the rise of Mahayana: in the witness of these scriptures to the particular form of experience in which the whole development originates and has its life.[173] And the "crown of Mahayana scripture" in this respect is the *Saddharma-Pundarika*.[174]

Of course, to realize this pre-eminence of the Lotus Sutra and to gain access to its meaning, an inner affinity or sense for its nature is the first requisite. Wach attributes the neglect of Mahayana in German Buddhist scholarship to the general absence of any affinity for it. The subjective, individualistic tenor of the Theravada corresponds more nearly to the German character. (The French are better attuned to Mahayana, he says, citing the work of de la Vallée-Poussin.)[175]

The objective study of the text presents few difficulties. It is not necessary to turn to the sources in the original languages, since the available translations offer no very great obstacles to the reader even if he is not well-versed in the Buddhist literature.[176] All that is required of the reader is flexibility and receptivity, an inner composure and the ability to think and feel with the writing; the style of thought and speech will then be mastered. The Sutra is often repetitive and tiresome, but if we only take the trouble to familiarize ourselves with the style it will no longer be an obstacle. We must gain "inner relationship to this whole world" in order to grasp the "inner necessity" which rules the construction of the Sutra as an organic whole.[177] Its linguistic forms and their significance will then become clear.

This Sutra takes the form of a narrative of an occasion

upon which the Buddha instructed his followers. It is composed
of long sections which set the stage for each segment of teaching, on the grandest possible scale: the Buddha is heard, wor-
shipped, and exalted by myriads of beings in countless worlds,
and his teaching is accompanied by signs and wonders throughout
the universe. Between these sections are passages, hardly less
impressive, which recount his teaching. Interspersed among
these are a number of stories or parables illustrating the
teaching. The intent of the long descriptive sections, says
Wach, is to create a "numinous" atmosphere, a tone which pervades the Sutra.[178] The heart of the Sutra, however, is the
parable: "Here we encounter genuine wisdom, genuine goodness,
genuine piety."[179] The content is eternally human: the parables
have the power to speak to anyone.

In the general expressions of the numinous and in the parables, we may recognize the genuine character and "spirit" of the
Sutra and of Mahayana itself. The experience of the Holy, as
Otto described it, is the central mode of apprehension of ultimate reality which comes to expression in this text. The central experience of Mahayana, according to Wach, is the experience that God exists.[180] This experience is what the text as
a whole conveys. From its parables, we may discern more clearly the form of that experience and the "idea" which accompanies
it: it is the experience and idea of divine grace, of God's
gracious help to his own creatures.[181] To this center, then,
everything else in the Sutra and in Mahayana is related: the
concept of the Buddha's nature, the idea of man, the ethical
precepts--all thought is determined by, and finds its significance in, this single spirit. Wach only sketches a few of
these relationships, but his book is not a commentary, and he
has accomplished his task by locating the spirit of the text.
By that very programmatic generality, Wach's treatment of the
Sutra seems to reveal the basic structure of his approach to
interpretation.

Interestingly, it is Wach's approach to the practice of
interpretation, and its relationship to his theoretical work,
which seems to have provoked the most sharp criticism. One
student of Buddhism has charged that Wach's treatment of that
and other religions has no real methodology. He writes: "Wach

does not distinguish the prerequisite attitudes of the investigator sufficiently from the operational procedure. In fact, he seems unaware of the need for operational method."[182] It is as if Wach's procedure were to match bits of data from religious documents to preconceived attitudes and schemata concerning the material, with their apparent "fit" being the only justification. The forms and assumptions which Wach brings to the material, not the data and their own meaningful structure, seem to determine his interpretations. The critic concludes: "Wach's liberal, benign and perceptive work is in fact a *Religionslehre*, a doctrine rather than a discipline."[183]

In a similar vein, other critics have remarked upon the "natural theology" which is implicit in Wach's treatment of interpretation.[184] Perhaps his eventual willingness to admit the possibility of a natural theology based in the comparative study of religions was an acknowledgement of that fact. Certainly Wach never intended to conceal his presuppositions. Theology and understanding, in his accounts of both, have the same starting-point: religious experience. It is from religious experience that all religious expression, including theology, develops; and it is from this experience also (or at least from a sense or capacity for the experience, from a recognition of the experience) that any valid comprehension of religious expression must begin. Wach presupposes explicitly that there is a delimitable and unitary phenomenon called "religious experience," with certain universal characteristics; and he presupposes that some form of this experience is at the heart of every religious text, and gives coherence to every religion. If it were not so, understanding would be--theoretically--impossible.

But these presuppositions are dubious, or at any rate dubitable.[185] They require some kind of transcendental support, as Wach clearly knew: hence his discussion of the "metaphysical decision." It is a decision with far-reaching implications. One treatment of Wach's work concludes a generally favorable evaluation with this admission: "If this kind of metaphysical position were judged as untenable one would want to reconstruct Wach's theory of religious experience. But for investigators of religion who can concur with what Wach calls his 'metaphysical decision,' his scientific theory presents itself as an instrument of unparalleled refinement."[186]

There is the difficulty--or at least one difficulty--with Wach's hermeneutical treatment. Those who cannot "concur" with any such decision may find Wach's work interesting as an interpretation of religion, but will have difficulty accepting it as a foundation for inquiry. Among them is one of Wach's successors at Leipzig, Kurt Rudolph. He holds that to require of the scholar a "sense for religion" is to transgress the bounds of scientific investigation.[187] Wach was therefore unable to realize his early vision of a strict separation between normative and descriptive treatments of religion; his concept of religious experience introduces a normative element, which Rudolph believes cannot be retained. "For: religion is not the *source*, but the *object* of research in the history of religions."[188]

Even if Rudolph's objection were overruled, and it were granted that only the "religious" person can understand religion, difficulties would remain. Many "religious" people would deny that there is any one basic experience--or indeed any significant element at all--which is common to all those phenomena which happen to be labelled "religious." Even within one "religion" there may be such wide differences as to make any assertion about a common spirit or character either false or meaningless. Wach's usual response to these suggestions of discontinuity among religions is to classify them as normative theological statements, in which a religious group is trying to express its sense of uniqueness; a broader, more dispassionate view may nevertheless place the religion in the proper context for interpretation.[189] Here he must posit, as a precondition for understanding, a model which is unacceptable to those whose "religion" is the object of understanding. In defense of it, he may refer to a metaphysical standpoint which may be even less acceptable to them. Both the model of "religion" and the metaphysical foundation upon which it rests are questionable, at least, from a number of viewpoints.

Wach's hermeneutical effort is governed by the practical aim of providing guidance for the interpretation of religious data. His primary interest is in the problem of understanding, not in the construction of theory, in religious studies. Yet it appears that his fundamental paradigm of the operation of

understanding requires him to assimilate the practice of interpretation to a dominant theoretical construct, rather than
enabling him to deal reflectively with the practical dimensions
of the activity of interpreting religious texts, utterances,
and phenomena. The roots of this conflict must be studied more
closely.

NOTES TO CHAPTER II

1. Joachim Wach, "Religious Commitment and Tolerance," *Understanding and Believing: Essays by Joachim Wach*, ed. Joseph M. Kitagawa (N.Y.: Harper & Row, 1968), p. 143.

2. See Kurt Rudolph, *Die Religionsgeschichte an der Leipziger Universität und die Entwicklung der Religionswissenschaft*, Sitzungsberichte der Sächsichen Akademie der Wissenschaften zu Leipzig, Philologisch-historische Klasse, 107:1 (Berlin: Akademie-Verlag, 1962), pp. 137-139.

3. Joachim Wach, *Religionswissenschaft: Prolegomena zu ihrer wissenschaftstheoretischen Grundlegung* (Leipzig: J. C. Hinrichs, 1924), p. 68.

4. Joachim Wach, "Und die Religionsgeschichte? Eine Auseinandersetzung mit D. Paul Althaus," *Zeitschrift für Systematische Theologie*, VI (1929), pp. 492-494.

5. Joachim Wach, "'Nur.' Gedanken über den Psychologizismus," *Zeitschrift für Missionskunde und Religionswissenschaft*, XXXIX (1924), pp. 210-212. A further attack, directed specifically against Freud, appears in Wach's article, "Das religiöse Gefühl," in the symposium *Das Problem der Kultur und die ärztliche Psychologie*, Vortrage des Instituts für Geschichte der Medizin an der Universität Leipzig, IV (Leipzig: Thieme, 1931), pp. 16-18.

6. Wach, "'Nur.' Gedanken über den Psychologizismus," p. 215.

7. The three volumes of *Das Verstehen* were subtitled, respectively: *Die grossen Systeme; Die theologische Hermeneutik von Schleiermacher bis Hofmann;* and *Das Verstehen in der Historik von Ranke bis zum Positivismus*.

8. On this inadequacy in Betti, see the critique by Neils Thulstrup, "An Observation Concerning Past and Present Hermeneutics," *Orbis Litterarum*, XXII (1967), esp. pp. 30, 37.

9. Joachim Wach, *Einführung in die Religionssoziologie* (Tübingen: J. C. B. Mohr [Paul Siebeck], 1931).

10. Joachim Wach, *Sociology of Religion* (Chicago: University of Chicago,Press, 1944).

11. *Ibid.*, ch. 1, esp. pp. 5-6.

12. Richard W. Scheimann has discussed the development of Wach's thought on this theme in his *Wach's Theory of the Science of Religion* (Ph.D. dissertation, University of Chicago, 1963), pp. 26-31.

13. Wach, *Religionswissenschaft*, pp. 37-38, 67-68.

14. Wach, "Religious Commitment and Tolerance," p. 145. Wach wrote several articles during this period regarding the

relationship of the history of religions to theology; he
had become more congenial to the idea of a constructive
relationship than he had been at first (see e.g. *Religionswissenschaft*, p. 124), because the terms of the relationship were differently envisioned.

15. This is suggested in the concluding chapter of Joachim
Wach, *Types of Religious Experience: Christian and Non-
Christian* (Chicago: University of Chicago Press, 1951),
pp. 288-289.

16. These relationships are emphasized by Thomas F. O'Dea,
*Sociology and the Study of Religion: Theory, Research,
Interpretation* (N.Y.: Basic Books, 1970), pp. 213-215,
257-261.

17. In both cases, Wach may have confessed a greater debt than
actually existed; the situation may have been more nearly
one of agreement on certain points than of any considerable
dependence. Wach's independent arrival at a position similar to Otto's seems to be suggested, for instance, in
Wach's review of Otto's *Indiens Gnadenreligion und das
Christentum*: Joachim Wach, "Ein Meisterstück der vergleichenden Religionsforschung," *Die Christliche Welt*,
XLV (1931), pp. 20-25, esp. p. 21.

18. Scheimann, *Wach's Theory of the Science of Religion*, p.
61. Gadamer remarks that Wach's *Das Verstehen* "rests
wholly within Dilthey's horizon" (*Wahrheit und Methode*,
p. 171).

19. In their reviews of Wach's posthumously published *The
Comparative Study of Religions*, both Seymour Cain (in *The
Journal of Religion*, XL [1960], pp. 47-49) and Kurt
Rudolph (in *Theologische Literaturzeitung*, LXXXIX [1964],
pp. 346-349) criticize the practice of seemingly indis-
criminate citation of references as a major weakness of
the book.

20. E.g. Joseph Kitagawa in his introduction to Joachim Wach,
The Comparative Study of Religions, ed. Joseph M. Kitagawa (N.Y.: Columbia University Press, 1958), p. xl;
Hans-Joachim Schoeps, in "Joachim Wach--In Memoriam,"
Zeitschrift für Religions- und Geistes-geschichte, IX
(1957), p. 368. In a review of Wach's *Types of Religious
Experience* (*Anglican Theological Review*, XXXV [1953], pp.
277-278), Noah E. Fehl compares him to Clement--with the
corresponding strengths and weaknesses in this respect.

21. Joachim Wach, *Der Erlösungsgedanke und seine Deutung*,
Veröffentlichungen des Forschungsinstituts für ver-
gleichende Religionsgeschichte an der Universität
Leipzig, VIII (Leipzig: J. C. Hinrichs, 1922), ch. 1.
Cf. Wilhelm Dilthey, "Die Typen der Weltanschauung und
ihre Ausbildung in den metaphysischen Systemen," *Gesam-
melte Schriften*, VII, ed. B. Groethuysen (Leipzig: B. G.
Teubner Verlag, 1931), pp. 77-78, 84-87.

22. Wach, *Religionswissenschaft*, p. 30.

23. Bultmann, "The Problem of Hermeneutics," p. 234.

24. An overview is given in the introduction to Wach, *Das Verstehen*, II, esp. pp. 37-44. Scheimann, *Wach's Theory of the Science of Religion*, stresses the prominence of the "great tradition" theme in Wach's historical thought.

25. Bultmann, "The Problem of Hermeneutics," p. 234.

26. See, for example, Wilfred C. Smith's review of Wach's *Types of Religious Experience* in *The Journal of Religion*, XXXIII (1953), pp. 303-304, and the review of Wach's *The Comparative Study of Religions* by E. O. James in *Church Quarterly Review*, CLX (1959), pp. 533-534. Smith says that Wach's writing "lacks decision" and is inconclusive; James, that the book under review is well-informed, but makes no particular contribution to knowledge in either method or content.

27. See Kitagawa's remarks in this vein in his introduction to Wach, *Understanding and Believing*, p. viii.

28. "Since the death of Joachim Wach, the complicated onto-logical and epistemological baggage of philosophical phenomenology has been left far behind, and the philo-sophical non-technical masses are fair game for initiation into the rites of phenomenology of religion," observes Willard G. Oxtoby, "*Religionswissenschaft* Revisited," *Religions in Antiquity: Studies in Memory of Erwin Ramsdell Goodenough*, ed. Jacob Neusner, Studies in the History of Religions, Supplements to *Numen*, XIV (Leiden: E. J. Brill, 1968), pp. 595-596. The process of simplification actually began long before Wach's death, and under his sanction.

29. E.g. by Joseph M. Kitagawa, in his "Primitive, Classical, and Modern Religions: A Perspective on Understanding the History of Religions," *The History of Religions: Essays on the Problem of Understanding*, ed. Joseph M. Kitagawa, Essays in Divinity, I (Chicago: University of Chicago Press, 1967), pp. 39-65.

30. Kees W. Bolle, "Jan de Vries (1890-1964)," *History of Religions*, V (1965), p. 176; Mircea Eliade, "History of Religions and a New Humanism," *History of Religions*, I (1961), p. 2, and more recently Eliade's "On Understanding Primitive Religions," *Glaube, Geist, Geschichte: Festschrift für Ernst Benz zum 60. Geburtstag am 17. November 1967*, ed. Gerhard Müller and Winfried Zeller (Leiden: E. J. Brill, 1967), pp. 498-505.

31. E.g. by Charles H. Long, "Prolegomena to a Religious Hermeneutic," *History of Religions*, VI (1967), pp. 254-264.

32. Wach, *Das Verstehen*, III, p. 4.

33. Wach, *Das Verstehen*, I, pp. 1-2.

34. *Ibid.*, pp. 5-6.

35. *Ibid.*, pp. 12-30; cf. Dilthey, "Die Entstehung der Hermeneutik," esp. pp. 323-329.

36. Wach, *Das Verstehen*, II, pp. 37-38.

37. A great many errors might have been avoided in the course of the development of both hermeneutics and *Religionswissenschaft*, Wach believes, if their initial close relationship as exemplified by Herder has been maintained. *Ibid.*, pp. 65-67.

38. Wilhelm Dilthey, *Leben Schleiermachers*, II, ed. Martin Redeker (Göttingen: Vanderhoek & Ruprecht, 1966), p. 649.

39. Wach, *Das Verstehen*, I, p. 21.

40. In addition to his frequent references to Herder in *Das Verstehen*, Wach defends his centrality in "Zur Beurteilung Friedrich Schlegels," *Philosophischer Anzeiger*, IV (1929), pp. 13-26, esp. p. 24.

41. Wach, *Das Verstehen*, II, pp. 37-42.

42. *Ibid.*, pp. 251-252.

43. H. A. Hodges, *Wilhelm Dilthey: An Introduction* (London: Routledge & Kegan Paul, 1944), p. 13. Wach's review of this book (*The Journal of Religion*, XXVI [1946], pp. 74-75) is wholly favorable.

44. Wach, *Das Verstehen*, I, p. 85.

45. *Ibid.*, I, pp. 8-9; II, pp. 253-254.

46. *Ibid.*, I, p. 12.

47. *Ibid.*, II, pp. 94-95.

48. *Ibid.*, I, p. 246, n. 1.

49. *Ibid.*, I, p. 10. In his article, "Verstehen," *Die Religion in Geschichte und Gegenwart*, 2nd ed., V (Tübingen: J. C. B. Mohr [Paul Siebeck], 1931), col. 1571, Wach states that the act of understanding is certainly a matter which can be epistemologically considered. But the interests of the philosopher, and of the psychologist, will differ from those of the hermeneutical theorist. See also *Das Verstehen*, II, p. 4, n. 1.

50. Wach, *Das Verstehen*, II, p. 4.

51. *Ibid.*, I, p. 11.

52. *Ibid.*, II, pp. 23, 56.

53. Joachim Wach, "Zur Hermeneutik heiliger Schriften," *Theologische Studien und Kritiken*, CII (1930), pp. 281-282.

54. Wach, *Das Verstehen*, II, pp. 16-17.

55. Wilhelm Dilthey, "Das Verstehen anderer Personen und ihrer Lebensäusserungen," *Gesammelte Schriften*, VII, ed. B. Groethuysen (Leipzig: B. G. Teubner Verlag, 1927), p. 217. See Wach, *Das Verstehen*, II, p. vi.

56. Wach, *Das Verstehen*, I, pp. 11-12.

57. *Ibid.*, pp. 192-194. The philologist F. A. Wolf cited the fact as an argument against hermeneutical theory; Boeckh granted it readily as a clarification of the distinction between hermeneutics and interpretative practice.

58. *Ibid.*, III, pp. 300-301.

59. Schleiermacher, *Hermeneutik*, p. 80.

60. Dilthey, "Die Entstehung der Hermeneutik," p. 319; cf. Wach's formulation in *Das Verstehen*, I, p. 5.

61. Wach, *Das Verstehen*, II, pp. 14-15.

62. *Ibid.*, I, p. 5; II, p. 15.

63. *Ibid.*, I, p. 108. (See Schleiermacher, *Hermeneutik*, p. 31.)

64. In Joachim Wach, "On Teaching History of Religions," *Pro Regno Pro Sanctuario*, ed. W. J. Kooiman and J. M. van Veen (Nijkerk: G. F. Callenbach, 1950), pp. 527-528, the reader is referred to the whole of *Das Verstehen* in confirmation of this point.

65. Wach, *Das Verstehen*, I, p. 79.

66. *Ibid.*, III, pp. 13-14.

67. Dilthey, "Die Entstehung der Hermeneutik," p. 319.

68. Wach, *The Comparative Study of Religions*, p. 11.

69. Wach, *Das Verstehen*, II, p. 74.

70. Wach, "Zur Hermeneutik heiliger Schriften," p. 283.

71. See e.g. his article, "Verstehen," col. 1573, and Joachim Wach, "The Interpretation of Sacred Books," *Journal of Biblical Literature*, LV (1936), p. 63.

72. Joachim Wach, "On Understanding," *The Albert Schweitzer Jubilee Book*, ed. A. A. Roback (Cambridge, Mass.: Sci-Art Publishers [1946]), p. 145.

73. Joachim Wach, "The Place of the History of Religions in the Study of Theology," *Types of Religious Experience*, pp. 28-29. In "Das Verstehen anderer Personen und ihrer Lebensäusserungen," Dilthey distinguishes between "elementary" and "higher" forms of understanding, apparently an adaptation of Schleiermacher's distinction between grammatical and psychological interpretation. The

elementary is a grasp of the conventional meanings of words and sentences; the higher is an understanding of the unity of mental life out of which a given expression arises (pp. 207-213). Wach's "integral comprehension" is akin to Dilthey's higher understanding, though Wach would not separate it so sharply from the grammatical, nor identify it so exclusively with the psychological, as Dilthey seems to do. For Wach it is an integrative ideal, as his choice of terms implies.

74. Joachim Wach, "The Meaning and Task of the History of Religions (Religionswissenschaft)," *Understanding and Believing*, p. 136. Wach, *Religionswissenschaft*, p. 31.

75. Wach, *Das Verstehen*, I, p. 11.

76. *Ibid.*, II, p. 4.

77. *Ibid.*, I, p. 51.

78. Wach, *The Comparative Study of Religions*, p. 11.

79. Wach, *Das Verstehen*, I, pp. 43-44.

80. Wach, "The Meaning and Task of the History of Religions (Religionswissenschaft)," p. 131.

81. Wach, *Das Verstehen*, II, pp. 9-10.

82. One of the strengths of Dilthey's approach to religion, according to Wach, was his instinctive rejection of rationalism as a block to any real comprehension of religious phenomena. Joachim Wach, "Wilhelm Dilthey über 'Das Problem der Religion,'" *Zeitschrift für Missionskunde und Religionswissenschaft*, XL (1925), p. 68.

83. Wach, *Das Verstehen*, II, p. 90.

84. *Ibid.*, p. 10.

85. Joachim Wach, "Zur Methodologie der allgemeinen Religionswissenschaft," *Zeitschrift für Missionskunde und Religionswissenschaft*, XXXVIII (1923), pp. 45-46.

86. Wach, *Das Verstehen*, III, pp. 236-238.

87. *Ibid.*, II, p. 12.

88. Wach, *Religionswissenschaft*, pp. 27-28; "Zur Methodologie der allgemeinen Religionswissenschaften," p. 46.

89. Wach, *Das Verstehen*, II, p. 19.

90. Wach, "Zur Hermeneutik heiliger Schriften," p. 286; "Und die Religionsgeschichte?", p. 493.

91. Joachim Wach, "Die Geschichtesphilosophie des 19. Jahrhunders und die Theologie der Geschichte," *Historiche Zeitschrift*, CXLII (1930), p. 13. Cf. *Das Verstehen*, II, pp. 9-10.

92. Wach, *Das Verstehen,* II, pp. 9-10.

93. Joachim Wach, "Religionswissenschaft," *Die Religion in Geschichte und Gegenwart,* 2nd ed., IV (Tübingen: J. C. B. Mohr [Paul Siebeck], 1930), cols. 1956-1957.

94. Wach, *Religionswissenschaft,* pp. 143-147.

95. Wach, "Verstehen," col. 1572.

96. Wach, *Das Verstehen,* II, p. 16.

97. *Ibid.,* II, p. 22.

98. Dilthey, "Das Verstehen anderer Personen und ihrer Lebensäusserungen," pp. 208, 214-216; cf. Wach, *Religionswissenschaft,* pp. 194-196.

99. Wach, *Religionswissenschaft,* p. 154. The conception of understanding as the repetition of the creative process, popular since Ast, misleads us into a "psychologizing" of the work and a neglect of its content (Wach, *Das Verstehen,* I, pp. 53-54).

100. Wach, "Zur Methodologie der allgemeinen Religionswissenschaft," p. 46.

101. Wach, "On Understanding," p. 142.

102. On the influence of the theme see Wach, *Das Verstehen,* I, pp. 35, 183-184.

103. Wach, *Das Verstehen,* II, p. 255.

104. Jean Séguy, "Expérience religieuse et sociologie des religions: Joachim Wach sociologue des religions," *Archives de sociologie des religions,* VII (1962), p. 32.

105. Kimmerle, "Hermeneutische Theorie oder ontologische Hermeneutik," p. 120.

106. Speculation and Hegelian philosophy are not identical, Wach reminds his readers, despite the tendency of friends and foes alike to equate them (*Das Verstehen,* II, p. 286).

107. E.g. in "On Understanding," p. 132; "Und die Religionsgeschichte?", p. 491; "Verstehen," col. 1571.

108. Wach, *Das Verstehen,* III, p. 11.

109. *Ibid.,* II, pp. 71-73.

110. *Ibid.,* II, pp. 288-289.

111. Wach, *The Comparative Study of Religions,* pp. 15-19.

112. H. A. Hodges, *The Philosophy of Wilhelm Dilthey* (London: Routledge & Kegan Paul, 1952), p. 133.

113. *Ibid.,* pp. 196, 213-224.

114. Wach, *Der Erlösungsgedanke und seine Deutung*, pp. 9-11.

115. Wach, "The Meaning and Task of the History of Religions (Religionswissenschaft)," pp. 134-135.

116. Intramural disputes are occasionally noted, but are kept outside the bounds of the hermeneutical discussion, in Wach's treatment (e.g. in *Das Verstehen*, I, pp. 140-141).

117. Wach *The Comparative Study of Religions*, p. 18. His criticism of Heidegger may be recalled in this connection.

118. Wach, "On Understanding," pp. 134, 141; *Das Verstehen* p. 261; *The Comparative Study of Religions*, p. 18.

119. Wach, *Das Verstehen*, I, pp. 36-37, 140-141; II, p. 165.

120. Wach, "On Understanding," p. 134. Earlier, Wach had complained of the lack of precision in the usage of the term "*Geist*" in hermeneutical history (*Das Verstehen*, II, pp. 71-72), but here he seems willing to turn that ambiguity to good advantage.

121. Dilthey, "Die Entstehung der Hermeneutik," pp. 329-330.

122. Wach, "On Understanding," p. 141. Dilthey would not have found such hypotheses acceptable (see Hodges, *The Philosophy of Wilhelm Dilthey*, p. 78); but Wach does not rely on them in any case.

123. Wach, *Religionswissenschaft*, p. 158.

124. Wach, "The Meaning and Task of the History of Religions (Religionswissenschaft)," p. 135; "On Understanding," pp. 141-142.

125. Wach, "The Interpretation of Sacred Books," p. 61.

126. Wach, *Das Verstehen*, I, pp. 250-256.

127. Wach, *Religionswissenschaft*, pp. 155-157; cf. Dilthey, "Das Verstehen anderer Personen und ihrer Lebensäusserungen," p. 214.

128. Wach, *Religionswissenschaft*, pp. 36-37, 149-153; "Verstehen," col. 1573.

129. Wach, "Wilhelm Dilthey über 'Das Problem der Religion,'" pp. 68-71; "Das Religiöse Gefühl," p. 23.

130. Wach, *The Comparative Study of Religions*, p. 39.

131. Joachim Wach, "Bemerkungen zum Problem der 'externen' Würdigung der Religion," *Zeitschrift für Missionskunde und Religionswissenschaft*, XXXVIII (1923), p. 166.

132. Joachim Wach, "Rudolf Otto and the Idea of the Holy," *Types of Religious Experience*, pp. 218-221.

133. Joachim Wach, "The Self-Understanding of Modern Man,"

Understanding and Believing, p. 7.

134. Joachim Wach, "Universals in Religion," *Types of Religious Experience,* pp. 32-33; *The Comparative Study of Religions,* pp. 30-37.

135. Joachim Wach, "The Idea of Man in the Near Eastern Religions," *Types of Religious Experience,* p. 64; "Universals in Religion," pp. 39-40.

136. Wach, *Sociology of Religion,* p. 56.

137. *Ibid.,* pp. 45-46.

138. *Ibid.,* pp. 19, 25.

139. Joachim Wach, "Idee und Realität in der Religionsgeschichte," *Zeitschrift für Theologie und Kirche,* VIII (1927), pp. 336-338, 349. After such an account, Wach's suggestion that Hegel's characterization of religions "may still be read with profit" (*Sociology of Religion,* p. 45) comes as no great surprise.

140. Wach, *Sociology of Religion,* pp. 37, 56.

141. *Ibid.,* p. 376.

142. In another connection, Wach quotes Droysen's formula: "So sollst Du sein, denn so verstehe ich Dich" (On Understanding," p. 146.

143. Wach, "The Interpretation of Sacred Books," pp. 62-63.

144. Wach, "Wilhelm Dilthey über 'Das Problem der Religion,'" p. 80. See Wilhelm Dilthey, "Das Problem der Religion," *Gesammelte Schriften,* VI, ed. Georg Misch (Leipzig: B. G. Teubner,Verlag, 1924), pp. 288-305.

145. Wach, *Religionswissenschaft,* pp. 37-38, 187; *Sociology of Religion,* p. 14.

146. Joachim Wach, "The Problem of Truth in Religion," *Understanding and Believing,* p. 148.

147. Wach, *The Comparative Study of Religions,* pp. 11-13; "On Understanding," p. 144.

148. Wach, "On Understanding," pp. 142-143.

149. Wach, "The Interpretation of Sacred Books," p. 60.

150. Wach, "Universals in Religion," p. 34; see also *The Comparative Study of Religions,* p. 59. Elsewhere Wach admits the possibility of what he once calls "immediate comprehension of another's soul" (*Sociology of Religion,* pp. 44-45); but this is rare at best, and cannot be relied upon in interpretation.

151. Wach, *Das Verstehen,* I, pp. 247-249, 258-265.

152. *Ibid.*, I, pp. 97-101.

153. Wach, "The Interpretation of Sacred Books," p. 63.

154. Wach, *Religionswissenschaft*, p. 55.

155. Wach, *Das Verstehen*, II, pp. 69-70; *Religionswissenschaft*, pp. 70-71; *Sociology of Religion*, p. 15.

156. Wach, *Religionswissenschaft*, pp. 35-36; "The Problem of Truth in Religion," p. 150; "Universals in Religion," p. 30.

157. Wach, "Zur Methodologie der allgemeinen Religionswissenschaft," pp. 38-39.

158. Wach, *Der Erlösungsgedanke und seine Deutung*, pp. 35-39.

159. Henri Desroche, "Sociologie et theologie dans la typologie religieuse de Joachim Wach," *Archives de sociologie des Religions*, I (1956), pp. 48-49.

160. Wach, "Universals in Religion," p. 37; *Sociology of Religion*, pp. 60-61.

161. Wach, *Sociology of Religion*, p. 23.

162. *Ibid.*, pp. 20-22. Wach regards myth as *sui generis* as a constantly valid category of religious expression, and resists "demythologizing" as a movement which misunderstands the nature of its material (*The Comparative Study of Religions*, p. 66).

163. Wach, *Religionswissenschaft*, pp. 147-148; *Das Verstehen*, I, p. 233.

164. Joachim Wach, "Sociology of Religion," *Twentieth Century Sociology*, ed. Georges Gurvitch (N.Y.: Philosophical Library, 1945), p. 421.

165. Joachim Wach, *Die Typenlehre Trendelenburgs und ihr Einfluss auf Dilthey: Ein philosophie- und geistesgeschichteliche Studie*, Philosophie und Geschichte, 11 (Tübingen: J. C. B. Mohr [Paul Siebeck], 1926), p. 7.

166. Joachim Wach, "The Concept of the Classical in the Study of Religions," *Types of Religious Experience*, p. 56. It was Dilthey who saw that typology is a matter of experience as well as of intellect (Wach, *Die Typenlehre Trendelenburgs*, pp. 28-34).

167. Wach, "The Concept of the Classical," p. 55.

168. Wach, "The Interpretation of Sacred Books," pp. 62-63.

169. Kees W. Bolle, "Wach's Legacy: Reflexions on a New Book," *History of Religions*, X (1970), p. 83, defends Wach in this regard by citing his considerable knowledge of Mahayana Buddhism.

170. Joachim Wach, *Mahayana, besonders im Hinblick auf das Saddharma-Pundarika-Sutra: Eine Untersuchung über die religionsgeschichtliche Bedeutung eines heiligen Textes der Buddhisten* (München-Neubiberg: Schloss, 1925), p. 18.

171. *Ibid.*, pp. 14-15, 28, 34. Wach repeats his emphasis on the unity and "solidarity" of Mahayana in a later article, "The Study of Mahayana Buddhism," *Types of Religious Experience*, pp. 108-109.

172. Wach, *Mahayana*, p. 9.

173. *Ibid.*, pp. 30-31.

174. *Ibid.*, pp. 20-21.

175. *Ibid.*, p. 6.

176. *Ibid.*, pp. 9, 23. The available translations to which he refers are the English of Kern and the French of Burnouf.

177. *Ibid.*, pp. 9-12.

178. *Ibid.*, pp. 40-41.

179. *Ibid.*, p. 23.

180. *Ibid.*, p. 37: "die Erfahrnis, dass (ein) *Gott* ist."

181. *Ibid.*, pp. 37-39, 43.

182. Richard H. Robinson, in his review of Wach's *The Comparative Study of Religions, Canadian Journal of Theology,* VIII (1962), p. 58.

183. *Ibid.*, p. 59.

184. Desroche, "Sociologie et theologie dans la typologie religieuse de Joachim Wach," p. 47; Kurt Rudolph, review of Wach's *Vergleichende Religionsforschung* (translation of *The Comparative Study of Religions*), *Theologische Literaturzeitung,* LXXXIX (1964), pp. 347-348.

185. See H. Richard Niebuhr's review of Wach's *Sociology of Religion, Theology Today,* II (1945), pp. 409-410.

186. Scheimann, *Wach's Theory of the Science of Religion,* p. 270.

187. Rudolph, *Die Religionsgeschichte an der Leipziger Universität,* pp. 145-146.

188. Kurt Rudolph, "Leipzig und die Religionswissenschaft," *Numen,* IX (1962), p. 63.

189. See e.g. Wach, *The Comparative Study of Religions,* p. 28; "Und die Religionsgeschichte?", p. 494.

CHAPTER III

THE PROBLEM OF UNDERSTANDING

Is it true then that what Wach offers us is a doctrine rather than a discipline? Religious hermeneutics on his model does have a definite structural similarity to religious language itself. Hermeneutics and theology must both be rooted in and directed by religious experience, if hermeneutics is to "fit" its object and do it justice. And the elaboration of hermeneutics within the field of religious studies somehow parallels the course of theological reflection upon religious experience. The interpretation of any particular instance of religious language involves the recapitulation of its general possibilities as a type of religious expression, before its singular characteristics--always within the limits of its type--can be appreciated. This means that hermeneutics must give rise to an interpretative framework within which any particular religious phenomenon or expression can be assigned a place. As Wach found when he began to develop one in his later writings, such a framework may be pressed into service as a form of "natural theology" without the need for much revision in its structure.

Yet this hermeneutical framework is not "doctrine" in Wach's own sense of that term. It is not designed to serve any practical religious interest, though the possibility of its usefulness to future theological construction is recognized. Wach never surrendered the distinction between the descriptive nature of both hermeneutics and *Religionswissenschaft* and the normative interests of the theological and philosophical disciplines. Hermeneutics remains a "descriptive-understanding" concern.

The claim that the hermeneutical framework for the interpretation of religious phenomena is established by purely descriptive, "empirical" means may be difficult to sustain. To accept Wach's account, one must be willing to grant several points whose truth is not immediately obvious: that there is

a universally constant human nature, containing the capacity
for (that is, a latent form of) something called "religious experience"; that this religious experience, in all its forms, reflects a single "ultimate reality"; that religious experience
is the center of all true religion and constitutes the ultimate
meaning of all religious expression; that the authentic function of religious language is to express, communicate, and sustain religious experience. Both personal experience and an
impartial survey of man's religious history, according to Wach,
should convince us of the truth of these assertions; they *are*
obviously true.[1]

When Wach names personal experience and historical knowledge as the two paths to an awareness of the nature of religion, he reveals the circle of interpretation within which his
assertions are obvious and convincing; for personal experience
is, of course, the key to the meaning of the external evidence.
That is, historical religious phenomena are meaningful only insofar as they can be linked to religious experience; if they
did not bear testimony to religious experience, they could not
be recognized as religious at all. They could not be *understood*. Wach's plea for a balance between the empirical and the
a priori, and his warnings against a simple intuitionism or
"apriorism," are directed against any tendency to discard historical evidence and to lapse into anarchistic subjectivism in
interpretation. But there is no question that the *a priori* is
still the dominant force in interpretation for Wach. In fact,
the practice of interpretation seems to be largely a matter of
finding a way to reconcile the evidence of any given text or
phenomenon with the articulated "sense for religion" which one
is already supposed to possess. So long as the evidence is
not blatantly disregarded or contradicted, the requirements of
interpretation are basically satisfied once it has been plaus-
ibly associated with one's prior understanding of religion.
It is the nature of understanding itself which requires the
text or phenomenon to be taken in a certain way, and which
allows, or dictates, a theory of religion such as that which
Wach offers as an interpretative framework. Those who do not
share the framework apparently have not properly cultivated
the sense for religion, and are therefore simply incapable of
recognizing or understanding the material.

To call it "doctrine" may be technically incorrect from Wach's point of view, but it does appear that his treatment of religion has some features usually associated with doctrines in a broader sense (whether religious, philosophical, or ideological) and that these features are indispensable. The investigator is asked to give his assent to a number of statements concerning the nature of the material he wishes to investigate --this, in addition to the original "metaphysical decision" which admits him to the hermeneutical circle generally. It is difficult not to view these as normative statements. Not only do they direct the investigator's interpretation of the material, they also determine at the outset what is to be considered authentically "religious," thus delimiting his field. They are the skeleton of a system within which any possible religious expression may be placed.

At this point, are religious phenomena being treated as objects of an inquiry, or as illustrations of a thesis? Interpretation of specific phenomena is informed by the general account of religious understanding to such a degree that it is not always possible to draw a line between theory and interpretation.[2] Hermeneutics appears to differ from "doctrine," and "understanding" from "explanation," only in that when something is "understood" it is placed (we are told) in immediate human experience, rather than in a speculative system: it is recognized for what it is. The hermeneutical structure is intended to facilitate that sort of recognition; therefore it does not function as one theory or ideology in competition with others.

Much of Wach's work could be used to give support to the critical claim that *Verstehen* is an operation designed to satisfy a psychological need: it calms our curiosity and relieves our apprehension concerning an alien phenomenon, and contributes minimally, if at all, to the constructive investigation of the object. It relates the object somehow to subjective processes, rendering it meaningful by finding familiar terms in which to place it. The familiarity may easily be misplaced, however, since nothing guarantees that simply because an object can be understood in such a way, it is adequately or faithfully represented by the operation.[3] That which is really central or distinctive in a text--the Lotus Sutra, for example--may be overlooked because it is not "recognizable" on these terms.[4]

Why should the phenomenon of "recognition," vulnerable as
it is to such criticism, be elevated to such importance in interpretation? It is because, for Wach and for the tradition
he represents, it is definitely not merely a psychologically
satisfying operation. The interpreter is not shaping inert
material into patterns of his own design; he is seeking to realize a relationship which already exists latently between
himself and the object. Understanding does not create "familiarity" by a psychological technique. It depends upon, and reveals, an actual kinship.

Understanding is thus our only means of access to the interior of the object, to its true nature. The external and
superficial is not of first importance in interpretation. From
the start, our attention is drawn away from the concrete detail
of the text and is focused instead upon the process of understanding and upon its conditions or requirements in the situation at hand. How is the object of understanding to be
grasped? In pursuing this problem, general hermeneutics tends
finally to foresake any direct methodological responsibilities,
and to ally itself with epistemology or ontology in sustained
reflection upon the nature of understanding itself.[5]

In his compact history of the concept of "*Verstehen*,"
Karl-Otto Apel delineates a more or less natural and inevitable
"unfolding" of the concept in this direction, culminating in
the existential hermeneutics of Heidegger and his followers.[6]
Gradually the practical concerns of the textual interpreter
have been shed, and the study of understanding has been pursued
by these later thinkers for its intrinsic rather than its possible instrumental value. For Gadamer, for example, hermeneutical reflection is essentially "a meditation about a *praxis*
which is itself already a natural and sophisticated one." It
yields no immediate practical results, but only a general increase in our self-awareness and self-understanding, a widening of our horizon.[7] Concurring in this description of the
task, Richard Palmer suggests that the "mission of general hermeneutics" for the future should be a descriptive one, aiming
at "a phenomenology and ontology of the event of understanding."[8] This concentration upon the understanding of understanding does have some effect upon the effort to understand

texts, however, as Gadamer and Palmer readily acknowledge. The
practical outcome of general hermeneutics is "to clarify the
limitations of methodologies."[9] General hermeneutics itself is
not methodology; it does not guide practice; but by examining
the nature of understanding, it shows what is admissible and
sets some limits to what can possibly be achieved in understanding. It quiets the more extravagant claims of naive interpreters.

Among the extravagant claims which Gadamer attacks, it
will be recalled, is one which Wach himself advanced (and which
Betti has recently renewed): that "objectivity" (however qualified) is a desirable and attainable goal for understanding.
The ontology of understanding reveals that although texts and
other objects may contribute something to the concern of understanding, their status is literally peripheral: understanding
has to do with the meeting of horizons, not with any direct
contact of object and subject. The object as such remains at
a distance. Hermeneutics is not an instrument for textual interpretation, but a mode of thought in which reflection upon
the encounter of the horizons of reader and text may further
self-understanding.

A tendency to think of hermeneutics as edifying in this
way is not entirely absent from Wach's approach. Understanding,
whatever its object, is considered a principal means of human
development, and has a value beyond the particular interpretative situation. Nevertheless, the interpretative situation,
the concrete problem of interpreting texts and phenomena, was
always at the heart of Wach's concerns. When the attempt to
discover what is involved in understanding texts is transformed
into a philosophical "meditation" pursued for its own sake,
the authentic mission of hermeneutics, from Wach's point of
view, has been forsaken. Resistance to such a turn in the
hermeneutical discussion is evident in his treatment of the
relationship of hermeneutics to philosophy. He wants to distinguish the hermeneutical formulation of the question of understanding from both philosophical and psychological inquiries
into its nature.[10] Although he does not provide any detailed
theoretical elaboration of this distinction, it is operative
in his work. On the one hand, his explicit rejection of
Heidegger's hermeneutics is based on the conviction that

understanding must always have a definite object, and that hermeneutics is therefore not free to become a self-contained body
of thought but must always be oriented to the problems given in
the relationship of interpreter and object. On the other hand,
he believes that the process of understanding must be given
some transcendental basis, and this necessitates some philosophical admissions. He does not want *Verstehen* to be explained
away simply as a psychological phenomenon. True, he follows
Dilthey's example in locating the possibility of understanding
in the nature and structure of human personality; but, again
like Dilthey, he leans toward a philosophical rather than a
clinical examination of personality, and finds it to be a repository for the *a priori* elements which permit recognitive
encounters with outwardly strange phenomena.

One indication of his resistance to the absorption of hermeneutics into philosophy is just at this point, in the way he
deals with the necessary philosophical foundation for understanding. The very generality—the informality, almost—of
his philosophical commitments is an attempt to keep philosophical issues at a distance and in fact to exclude them from our
working field once they have made their requisite contribution.
Wach sought an approach to understanding which would not require the subordination of either interpreter or object to the
other, but would instead permit a genuine relationship between
them in their integrity. Philosophy is admitted to the realm
of hermeneutics only to serve as a guarantee for the possibility
of this relationship.

Such a use of philosophy is regarded by the followers of
Heidegger as illegitimate. Wach would seem to have accepted
as a satisfactory settlement the problematic situation in which
Dilthey found himself when he at last recognized the metaphysical implications of his attempt at "descriptive" psychology.
To Wach, this was evidence that metaphysics was inescapable.
He attempted therefore to defend its proper role in hermeneutics (e.g. by refusing to equate speculative metaphysics with
Hegelianism), and at the same time to put restrictions on its
involvement and authority by admitting only that minimum of
metaphysical statement which the history of hermeneutics had
shown to be necessary. The followers of Heidegger might argue
that if, instead of searching for this minimum, Wach had

examined the event of understanding itself more thoroughly, he might have found that the primal "happening" of understanding does not admit of distinctions of "objective" and "subjective," and that a term like "recognition," implying these two poles, is therefore out of place. The metaphysical guarantee for the recognitive process is not only unwarranted but meaningless.

It is difficult to imagine what sort of rebuttal Wach might be able to make to this charge. He devoted very little attention to the "phenomenology" of understanding, in keeping with his circumscription of the hermeneutician's interest in the question. Yet he believed (and here he epitomized the tradition for which he spoke) that correct interpretation depends upon, and is justified by reference to, the proper performance of the understanding process. This process, so mysterious and so contingent upon hidden factors in the human psyche, is the treasure whose protection is the responsibility of hermeneutics. Wach chose accordingly to respect its mystery and to attend to its security. His refusal to provide a comprehensive account of the process did not have the intended effect of diminishing the issue and preventing the ascendancy of philosophical influence over hermeneutics, however. It only left a gap which more recent thinkers are only too willing to fill--incidentally undermining the ideal of integral, objective understanding whose vindication was Wach's aim.[11]

By stressing the centrality of the understanding-event, while excluding a scrutiny of that event from the proper business of hermeneutics, Wach appears to have left himself vulnerable to attack from two sides. Other students of religion raise serious questions about the "objectivity" his approach provides. Its price is too great: reliance on the religious *a priori* and on an interpretative framework built upon it may lead to misrepresentation and distortion of the object, and the conviction that one has recognized the inner essence of the phenomenon may be only "misplaced familiarity." This criticism is not directed at the possibility of objective understanding, but rather at Wach's failure to do justice to that goal, and especially to deal with it in a way which is illuminating for the interpreter. The theoretical element in Wach's work displaces the sort of discussion of interpretation which might actually promote objective understanding.

From the other side, meanwhile, Wach's goal itself is under attack: "objectivity" is a false hope, as a calm and descriptive explication of the understanding-event will demonstrate. While one side finds Wach too "philosophical," the other side finds his philosophical involvement inadequate. Both sides question the usefulness of his metaphysical assumptions—the first because they interfere with an impartial examination of the religious data, the second because they obstruct an investigation of the phenomenon of understanding. Apart from this antipathy to metaphysics, the two sides have little in common, and exhibit intramural divisions as well. Those who advocate simply "listening" to a text, purging ourselves of all prior hermeneutical notions, seem considerably divided among themselves as to what "listening" involves (if we may judge by their practice where explicit assertions are lacking), and rarely hear the same thing.[12] In any case, they are in turn regarded as naive and unreflective by those who, with varying kinds and degrees of philosophical rigor, defend and describe understanding. The question of the nature of understanding has not been settled, and the coherent hermeneutical program which Schleiermacher hoped the careful study of understanding would bring has not arrived.

The difficulties we face in understanding "understanding" were acutely felt by a contemporary of Wach's who was at quite a distance from this hermeneutical discussion: Ludwig Wittgenstein. Born in Vienna in 1889, Wittgenstein went to England to study in 1908. There his interests moved from aeronautical engineering and mathematics to logic and philosophy, which he studied at Cambridge, principally with Bertrand Russell. Though he spent considerable time on the Continent from these early years through 1929, his investigations of "understanding" were carried on mainly from the mid-1930's until his death in 1951, and mainly in Cambridge. They were not inspired or influenced by the problems of the hermeneutical theorists, but rather formed part of a sustained inquiry into some difficulties created by the form of our "psychological verbs"--"meaning," "intending," "expecting," and others, as well as "understanding."[13]

Recently Wittgenstein's work has begun to attract the

interest of some of the hermeneutical thinkers. In his posthumously published writings, representing the entire period of
his later philosophy, they find evidence of his concern with
what they take to be traditionally "hermeneutical" concepts,
suggesting that his work might have something to contribute
to the hermeneutical discussion.[14] On the whole, however, they
seem disappointed at what they find: Wittgenstein is a poor substitute for Husserl or Heidegger. Gadamer finds space for a
brief mention of Wittgenstein in an article on phenomenology,
noting with approval his rejection of psychologism and his concentration on language as the medium of human existence. (The
legacy of Husserl's teacher Brentano in Vienna, Gadamer suggests,
may have affected Wittgenstein and prompted his development in
this direction.) But Wittgenstein lacks any ontology. He does
not deal with the "ground of language," and his philosophy is
consequently largely negative, sketchy and incomplete.[15] Karl-
Otto Apel's treatment of Wittgenstein, though more comprehensive
and sympathetic, leads to a similar comparison with similar results: Wittgenstein is attempting to lay a hermeneutical foundation; he shares Heidegger's interest in language and his rejection of psychological explanations of understanding; but his
work lacks an ontological or meta-linguistic basis, and needs
some sort of completion.[16] Walter Schulz, also agreeing with
Gadamer's remarks, believes that Wittgenstein's failure to go
more deeply into the linguistic situation and to study the e-
vent of understanding is responsible for a stiffness and nar-
rowness in his account of understanding. It may be adequate to
the requirements of mathematical or scientific discourse, but
it does not do justice--as Gadamer's account does--to the
subtler conditions of understanding in the humanities or in
ordinary conversation.[17]

Wittgenstein's work has been assigned an inferior and
hardly significant place in the hermeneutical "unfolding" of
understanding, if these preliminary reports from the Heideggerian sphere of influence are any reliable indication. At best,
Wittgenstein's writings may have a propaedeutic value: they
may serve to initiate readers in the Anglo-Saxon world into
the real complexities and profundity of language and its relationship to the existential situation, and thereby awaken a
sensitivity to the ontological problems dealt with more directly

and adequately by Heidegger.[18] But this is an optimistic
stance. A less generous critic, discounting the superficial
resemblances, may regard Wittgenstein's work as a "travesty,"
a "caricature" of phenomenology, a sort of "anti-philosophy"
to be cast out and separated from the authentic inquiry into
human existence.[19]

It may indeed prove more fruitful not to regard the points
of apparent similarity between Wittgenstein and the hermeneutical philosophers as evidence of any common intellectual an-
cestry or common intention.[20] But this does not mean that
Wittgenstein's work should then be repudiated or ignored. If
he was not making a poor attempt to do what the hermeneutical
thinkers do well, perhaps it would not be totally irrelevant
to look more closely at what he *was* doing. What he has to say
about "understanding" should be heard, even though this might
not fit readily into the mode of thought current in hermeneutical reflection. His observations might have a more significant impact on hermeneutics, in a broader sense, if they are
not immediately subordinated to that current mode of thought.

Such a subordination is certainly possible--that is not
the issue.[21] What is questionable is the wisdom of classifying Wittgenstein in that way rather than first following out
the direction of his investigations. That would in fact involve going quite a different direction from ontological meditation, and recasting the discussion.

The Grammar of "Understanding"

Wittgenstein remarks upon "understanding" with some fre-
quency in his later philosophical work--that is to say, in the
period represented chiefly by his *Philosophical Investigations*.[22]
Nowhere does "understanding" receive anything like an exhaustive
analysis; that would have been foreign to the spirit of Wittgenstein's approach, even if it were possible. Rather, he comes at
"understanding" by one route in one context, then returns to it
later by a different way, and continually re-introduces it in
different connections. He wanted to break the hold on us exercised by certain words and their attendant images, by destroy-
ing the illusion that these words are monoliths with inherent,
consistent meanings. "Philosophy is a battle against
the bewitchment of our intelligence by means of language," he

wrote.[23]

A frontal attack on a troublesome word may be a less effective means of disenchantment than a patient exposition of its versatility. Even that exposition must be carried out by a variety of procedures, for there is no single philosophical method which is useful for the solution of all our difficulties.[24] The ambiguous, uneven, and unsystematic character of language is reflected, not disguised, in Wittgenstein's work.

It would be a mistake, then, to suppose that the body of Wittgenstein's philosophy might serve as a new hermeneutical foundation--an alternative to Dilthey or Heidegger. His writing as it stands does not lend itself to that sort of use at all. A thorough discussion of the "content" of his philosophy, centering perhaps on familiar Wittgensteinian loci such as "language-games," might not be the best approach to an appreciation of the significance of his treatment of "understanding." A theory of understanding, synthesized from a collection of Wittgenstein's observations on the subject, would be an even less satisfactory use of the material. Wittgenstein opposed the notion that the aim of philosophical reflection is to advance theories of any kind. "There must not be anything hypothetical in our considerations," he wrote. "We must do away with all *explanation*, and description alone must take its place."[25]

Any writer's claim that he is simply describing the way things are, and not theorizing at all, may justly be regarded with some caution. (It may be recalled, for instance, that Gadamer makes a similar statement about the purely "descriptive" nature of his work when some of his conclusions are challenged.[26]) These different "descriptions" do not just cancel one another out and reveal the emptiness of that sort of statement, however, even though we may be tempted to interpret them in that way. Our skepticism should lead instead to a closer look at what is actually being done. How does Wittgenstein describe "understanding," and how is the description to be taken? Some attention to this question might prepare us to consider how Wittgenstein's treatment of "understanding" may impinge on the hermeneutical discussion.

The second part of the question should be addressed first, so that we might know what to do with an answer to the first part. We may begin by recognizing that Wittgenstein directs his attention toward "understanding," not toward understanding: his is a *conceptual* investigation, rather than a phenomenological one. "We are not analyzing a phenomenon (e.g. thought) but a concept (e.g. that of thinking), and therefore the use of a word," he wrote.[27] This distinction requires some qualification, but must be clearly maintained nonetheless. It does not imply that language can be separated from life or experience and dealt with independently. Wittgenstein suggests rather that language and human life are inseparably interwoven. "Commanding, questioning, recounting, chatting, are as much a part of our natural history as walking, eating, drinking, playing."[28] Language has no sense apart from "the rest of our proceedings."[29] It is organically related with our human activity into our form of life, and is inconceivable in isolation from it.[30]

That means at the same time that an investigation of our language is an investigation of human life. Conceptual or (as Wittgenstein sometimes called it) "grammatical" investigation is not a way of avoiding a more fundamental examination of, say, understanding itself. On the contrary: it is only by paying attention to the complex use of "understanding" that we can get anywhere near the fundamental issues involved in the traditional inquiry into "the nature of understanding." In discussing a concept with some features common to "understanding," Wittgenstein said: "One ought to ask, not what images are or what happens when one imagines anything, but how the word 'imagination' is used. But that does not mean that I want to talk only about words. For the question as to the nature of the imagination is as much about the word 'imagination' as my question is. And I am only saying that this question is not to be decided--neither for the person who does the imagining, nor for anyone else--by pointing; nor yet by a description of any process. The first question also asks for a word to be explained; but it makes us expect a wrong kind of answer."[31]

The question about the nature of understanding, as we have seen it presented in the hermeneutical discussion, leads us to try to look somehow for something by that name. That search has some important consequences. For the moment, two general results may be mentioned. First, this sort of inquiry encourages us to ignore the great variety and complexity in our use of a term such as "understanding," and to search instead for (as Wittgenstein says) "*one* comprehensive essence."[32] According to Wittgenstein, we have a natural "craving for generality" in our thinking; particularity tends to be domesticated and subsumed under unities with which we are more comfortable.[33] But language resists domestication. Already in 1915, Wittgenstein was noting: "Language is a part of our organism and no less complicated than it." "The conventions of our language are extraordinarily complicated."[34] We wish to escape from this untidiness into a realm where the course of our thought is unhampered by inconsistencies and stubborn exceptions. Yet to do so is to reject the very situations--the concrete cases of linguistic use--which might have helped us to see the organic relation of language and life, and to formulate a more appropriate question.[35] The desire for simplicity, even in the guise of a formal demand for "elegance" in thought, is a temptation to be resisted.[36]

The meaning of a term such as "understanding" is not to be found apart from the actual linguistic situations in which the word normally occurs; so we must look to these situations, rough and disconnected as they are, if we want to know about "understanding." "A meaning of a word," according to Wittgenstein, "is a kind of employment of it. For it is what we learn when the word is incorporated into our language."[37] This remark may be taken in conjunction with another which has been widely cited as representing Wittgenstein's basic account of meaning: "For a *large* class of cases--though not for all--in which we employ the word 'meaning' it can be defined thus: the meaning of a word is its use in the language."[38] But this is not an assertion about the location of meaning, as if meaning were to reside in the use of words rather than somewhere else. As Donald Gustafson observes, it is a remark about a meaning of the word "meaning." Generally, that is, when we ask about the meaning of a word we want to know how it is used.[39] The "meaning" is what we receive when we ask someone to explain the word in its employment.[40] As Wittgenstein put it: "The meaning of a word is what the explanation of the meaning explains."[41]

Of course, the process of explanation may be formally structured in such a way as to demand another sort of anwer. Generations of teachers have assailed the pupil's natural tendency, when asked for a definition of a word, to respond (for example), "'Understanding' is when. . . ." The pupil wants to tell how the word is used, how it is normally employed in his language. The teacher wants something more substantial: the meaning which the word expresses or represents. The teacher has good pedagogical reasons for requiring something more than the pupil's impressions concerning the word; the conventions of the language as a whole may contradict, and almost certainly transcend, the pupil's limited acquaintance with a word. But insofar as the teacher's demand tends to reinforce the notion that "meaning" is something attached permanently to a word, it is perhaps fortunate that the pupil's resistance is difficult to overcome.

"There is always the danger of wanting to find an expression's meaning by contemplating the expression itself, and the frame of mind in which one uses it, instead of always thinking of the practice. That is why one repeats the expression to oneself so often, because it is as if one must see what is looking for in the expression and in the feeling it gives one."[42] Here Wittgenstein is calling attention to a second general result of the sort of inquiry which takes the form of questions about the nature of, say, understanding or imagination. Not only does it make us expect a comprehensive and univocal answer; it also leads us to think that the answer should consist of a body of information concerning the thing represented by the term. This information seems remarkably elusive, and special methods of inquiry may be devised in an effort to extract it. "In order to get clear about the meaning of the word 'think' we watch ourselves while we think; what we observe will be what the word means! --But," Wittgenstein adds, "this concept is not used like that."[43] The form of the question has misdirected us. Assertions about the frame of mind or mental state accompanying our use of the term "understanding" will not help us, despite their appeal. When we need are *reminders* about the way the term is employed. This is in fact how Wittgenstein's description of "understanding" is to be taken: as a set of reminders about the concept. He said, "The work of the philosopher consists in assembling reminders for a particular purpose."[44] Frequently that purpose is disillusionment, though it is not limited to that. To be relieved of the search for "the wrong kind of answer" by being reminded of the actual employment of a term may be an enabling sort of disillusionment in itself.

Generally, the reminders one assembles do not constitute a complete description of the use of an expression, but that incompleteness is not necessarily a disadvantage. The inability to provide an exhaustive description does not indicate a weakness to be overcome, but is itself a reminder of the versatility of language. "We are not at all prepared for the task of describing the use of e.g. the word 'to think.' (And why should we be? What is such a description useful for?)"[45] An account which pretended to completeness would have the character of an assertion requiring defense, a thesis to be proved; and this would be out of keeping wiht the aim of reminding. Similarly, the reminders must not exhibit a degree of precision which does not exist in the linguistic situation itself. Our concepts are often vague, especially outside the artificially structured realms of scientific and technical discourse. They have "blurred edges." Even "concept" is a vague concept.[46] But we get along with them, finding the ambiguity no particular hindrance for ordinary purposes, but rather an advantage.[47] In any event, it would be futile to attempt to establish (even under the banner of "description") precise and exhaustive standards for our operations with language. There is always a vast chasm between whatever requirement we seem to discern, if we think in terms of such fixed standards, and actual linguistic practice. Besides, that requirement seems to be set by a preconceived notion of what our inquiry must yield--a precise and comprehensive body of data, as in an ideal science--rather than following an investigation of our real need.[48] One of the philosopher's tasks, according to Wittgenstein, is to find the *specific* problems and to treat each in an appropriate way, rather than indulging in general responses to idealized requirements.

His reminders are therefore not to be taken as the components of a system--as if one could gather them in and, by supplying some logical cement, construct the theory which is latent in these elements. (No doubt theories can be constructed from this material; but the theorists must take responsibility for what they create.) The reminders are often examples, either

borrowed or invented, which indicate uses of expressions.
Again, it is not best always to think of these examples as an
indirect means of explanation, as illustrations of a thesis
which could be more generally stated if we gave more thought
to it. The example may well be all we have, and it is enough.[49]
For Wittgenstein, as John Wisdom says, "examples are the final
food of thought."[50]

Interspersed with the examples and case investigations in
Wittgenstein's writings are observations which he sometimes
calls "grammatical remarks." Like the examples, they call our
attention to certain features of linguistic behavior, suggesting different ways of looking at specific linguistic situations
which might dissolve some difficulties they contain. These re-
remarks are no more to be generalized than the examples themselves, as if *they* were the conclusions, the principles, which
Wittgenstein finally advances. They too are only notes, reminders, about features of our language which generally escape
notice, but which we will certainly acknowledge once they are
brought to our attention.[51]

Wittgenstein called his investigation a grammatical one;
and his statements, grammatical statements or grammatical remarks, as distinct from, say, scientific, theoretical or experiential statements.[52] That designation, more than any
other, seems to determine the way in which his remarks on such
terms as "understanding" are intended to be taken. There may
be some question, however, as to how the designation "grammatical" itself is to be understood. In his notes on Wittgenstein's lectures in 1930-33, G. E. Moore reports that he defined "grammar" in its ordinary sense, although he conceded
that he was "making things belong to grammar, which are not
commonly supposed to belong to it."[53] Certainly he was using
it in a broader, less rigorous (and perhaps therefore more
common) sense than it is given in its technical employment in
linguistic studies.[54] Yet there is a certain austerity and
strictness of purpose which is preserved in his use of "grammar," so that the term appears singularly congenial to the
spirit of his investigations. Grammar is descriptive. "Grammar does not tell us how language must be construed in order
to fulfill its purpose, in order to have such-and-such an effect on human beings. It only describes and in no way explains

the use of language," Wittgenstein declares.[55] (The occurrence
of the word "explanation" in Moore's version of Wittgenstein's
definition should not obscure this point. About the same time,
or shortly thereafter (1933), Wittgenstein wrote: "Grammar
describes the use of words in language."[56])

Grammatical investigation is not concerned, then, with the
origins or bases of language, either historically or ontologi-
cally. Inquiries into the natural history of language may be
interesting and worthwhile, but they belong elsewhere.[57] A
grammatical question is not properly answered by any kind of
hypothesis, but only by a clarification of the use to which a
particular word or expression is put under particular circumstances. It is a question about meaning. For instance: "Asking whether and how a proposition can be verified is only a particular way of asking 'How d'you mean?' The answer is a contribution to the grammar of the proposition."[58] A grammatical
remark is a note on the use of language. This is where Wittgenstein may be taking the term "grammar" somewhat beyond its
normal technical bounds, for he is only marginally interested
in morphology or syntax--in the formal, intrinsic structure of
the language--but quite interested in what we *do* with language,
in linguistic practice.[59] As Richard Bell observes, for Wittgenstein, "the patterns which are formed by the total activity
of speaking, the whole environment of a language-situation, is
its grammar."[60] Such an inclusive notion is far from precise,
but it seems to serve Wittgenstein's purpose. Grammar is the
description of the use of language; and since "the *speaking* of
language is part of activity, or a form of life," grammatical
investigation as Wittgenstein pursues it involves going beyond
linguistic forms to an observation of language in action.[61]

Grammatical investigation reveals a remarkable dissonance
between linguistic forms and linguistic activity, in fact. The
forms lead us to expect similarities of function where there
are none; formal grammar sometimes creates illusions which seem
to exert great power over our ways of thinking. "When words in
our ordinary language have prima facie analogous grammars we
are inclined to try to interpret them analogously; i.e. we try
to make the analogy hold throughout."[62] One aim of grammatical
investigation in such cases is to clear away the misunderstand-
ings created by these superficial similarities, by drawing our

attention away from the formal grammar to the more flexible, situational grammar of linguistic use.[63] We move, he says, from "surface grammar" to "depth grammar."[64] The depth grammar, of course, is not to be found by looking more "deeply" into the word itself--that may have been the source of the difficulty-- but by taking account of the situation in which the word is immersed, the "deep" conventions which govern its use.[65] It is when we concentrate on the word or expression itself, as if fascinated by it, that we find ourselves puzzled. We imagine that there is something more to it than we usually recognize, and the elusiveness of whatever it is only heightens our sense that there is a mystery here requiring profound concentration for its discernment.[66] For example, "in our failure to understand the use of a word we take it as the expression of a queer *process*. (As we think of time as a queer medium, of the mind as a queer kind of being.)"[67] If the "something" remains beyond our powers of perception, it is simply ineffable, perhaps "spiritual" (*geistige*).[68]

The substantive forms of verbs seem to be especially susceptible to this sort of interpretation. "We predicate of the thing what lies in the mode of representing it," as Wittgenstein put it succinctly.[69] The problems which can thus be created by the forms of language are nowhere more clearly evident than in what he calls the "psychological verbs"--e.g. "imagining," "meaning," "thinking," "intending," "understanding."[70] These all appear to be the names of processes or states of mind; and many of our expressions containing these words reinforce that impression. But how is a state of mind to be understood? If we want to investigate imagination, for example, "the analysis oscillates between natural science and grammar."[71] Is it imagination or "imagination" which is at issue? Frequently the analysis comes to rest between the two: that is to say, in metaphysics. Metaphysics "obliterates the distinction between factual and conceptual investigation," says Wittgenstein.[72] The form of the language inclines us toward an empirical investigation of, say, "the understanding"; but this turns out to be strictly impossible--or, rather, we seem to lack the equipment to find what we are looking for. Observations of behavior, perhaps even records of brain-processes, do not yield what we have been led by the form of the inquiry

to expect: a description of a state of mind. We may turn to
metaphysics, then, to provide the link between language and
reality--to provide a realm in which, we hope, states of mind
can be described to our satisfaction. And here we lose sight
of the fact--if indeed we ever recognized it--that "states of
mind" are fundamentally *grammatical* constructions, and that it
is therefore a grammatical investigation which is most needed.[73]

Wittgenstein never denied that some uses of a concept (e.g.
"remembering") may be associated with "inner processes" which
may be directly experienced or studied as psychological phenomena. He only doubted that a study of such inner occurrences
would ever satisfy our question about what "remembering" is.
(In another connection, he wrote: "It shews a fundamental misunderstanding, if I am inclined to study the headache I have now
in order to get clear about the philosophical problem of sensa-
tion."[74] And yet the turn to grammar instead should not be interpreted as a denial of the existence of the pain.[75]) Physiological or psychological information about the remembering-
process is not what we need, even though it may be available.
"The impression that we wanted to deny something arises from
our setting our faces against the picture of the 'inner process.' What we deny is that the picture of the inner process
gives us the correct idea of the use of the word 'to remember.'
We say this picture stands in the way of our seeing the use of
the word as it is."[76] We must resist the superficial grammatical form which forces itself upon us here, and put aside the
"inner process," the experience which seems to go with the concept.[77]

Despite the fact that many of them are grammatically designated as "states," there are great differences among the
psychological verbs, as well as among various uses of the same
word. One way to recognize these differences and to appreciate
the variety of familiar uses is to ask ourselves how we learned
a particular word. Under what circumstances did we find it
appropriate to use its different forms in expressions? What
examples or paradigms seem most important as reference-points
for our use?[78] Did we, for example, first learn the nature of
the good, and then apply the adjective "good" to different
things? Did we become acquainted with the imagination and then,
on the basis of that information, learn to use the different

forms of "to imagine" properly? Rather, we just gradually
learned the sorts of circumstances in which a person might be
justified in saying, e.g., "That's good," or "I must have only
imagined it." We learn the role of such expressions in our
everyday talk, learning when--for example--it is appropriate
to assign a "state of mind" to ourselves or to others.

According to Wittgenstein, then, to understand the grammar
of a "state," we should ask (as indeed we had to learn): "What
counts as a criterion for anyone's being in such a state?"[79]
The criteria are often complex. Though we use them well enough,
it is not so easy to isolate them, and to provide a complete
list (which could amount to a complete grammatical description
of an expression) might exceed our ability as well as our needs.
Grammatical criteria are formed by, and found in, the use of the
language; they are not superimposed upon it from without, but,
like language itself, rest upon convention.[80] As Rogers
Albritton puts it, "A criterion for a given thing's being so
is something that can show the thing to be so and show by its
absence that the thing is not so; it is something by which one
may be *justified in saying* that the thing is so and by whose
absence one may be justified in saying that the thing is not
so."[81] That is, one is justified in one's use of an expression
only by what counts, in linguistic practice, as evidence for
the appropriateness of one's use. "Inner processes" generally
do not count. "An 'inner process' stands in need of outward
criteria," Wittgenstein notes.[82] The "actual transactions of
the language" are what appear in the account-books of grammar--
not the feelings which may accompany those transactions.[83]

Wittgenstein's reliance on linguistic convention as the
arbiter of our difficulties with such things as "psychological
verbs," his willingness to let grammar tell us what sort of
thing we are dealing with, appears to some interpreters to reveal his ontological presuppositions. If language rest upon
convention, then the "forms of life" in which those conventions
rest have the place of a "metaphysical ultimate" in Wittgenstein's thought, according to one critic.[84] To another, Wittgenstein is offering us "a linguistic 'Constitution Theory,'
in which language is not derived from the world of objects but
is somehow involved in the construction of objects."[85] We proceed to ontological questions only through an analysis of the

way in which reality is linguistically constituted.[86]

What Wittgenstein says is that in our use of words we must respect linguistic convention, because that is how language works. Language rests upon convention. If a word is to have meaning, we must commit ourselves to using it in particular ways consistently. In the lectures recorded by Moore, Wittgenstein said: "There is no use correlating noises to facts, unless we commit ourselves to using the noise in a particular way again-- unless the correlation has consequences."[87] The effectiveness of language ordinarily depends upon our willingness to partici- pate responsibly in the existing conventions of its use--for example, to observe the criteria for "imagining" or "remembering" under given circumstances, when we want to know about the mean- ing of these expressions.

Wittgenstein does not rule out the possibility of our agreeing on new conventions in some situations (for instance, when a more strict definition of a technical term would serve our interest); and justification may be offered for adopting the new criteria for a term.[88] Our everyday language, however, has not grown according to any particular plan. If we were called upon to give a justification beyond conventional sanction for our use of a term, we would not ordinarily be able to do so.[89] Our use is unpredictable, in that it cannot be inferred from the term itself or from its surface grammar, from its ety- mology or history. A convention is not necessarily based on anything; it has just grown up as a part of our life.[90]

Does it appear from this that Wittgenstein is trying to elevate our conventions or "forms of life" to some sort of onto- logical primacy? His discussion may contain some elements which might be harmonized with a "linguistic constitution the- ory," or with some other theory of the relation of language to reality.[91] But that act of harmonization, it would seem, would immediately remove Wittgenstein's remarks from their intended sphere of operation and put them into another context. Witt- genstein is talking about grammar, about the way language is used, and not about its ontological basis. Philosophy cannot give any foundation to language, he insists.[92] In one of his discussion of the "groundlessness" of our linguistic behavior, he anticipates the charge that he is granting language an ul- timate power over reality: "'So you are saying that human agreement decides what is true and what is false?' --It is what human beings *say* that is true and false; and they agree in the *language* they use. That is not agreement in opinions but in forms of life."[93] The conventions of language are not "pre-understandings," nor an accepted body of quasi-metaphysical propositions into which reality must be forced. Some features of *surface* grammar may incline us toward metaphysical prejudices which are hard to overcome, as Wittgenstein suggests.[94] But on the level of convention--that is, of the actual use of our language--our agreement does not predetermine the substance of our linguistic transactions ("what human beings *say*"), but rather makes it possible for us to say anything and be understood. It is an agreement in behavior, not in "opinions."[95]

Wittgenstein leaves speculation about the origins of linguistic conventions outside the scope of his interests, just as he refused to grant the study of psychological processes any place in a grammatical investigation. His work is not in any direct opposition to a phenomenological or psychological study of language. But he did not expect these studies to be of any more help in the treatment of essentially grammatical problems than similar studies of "mental states." The perplexities which arise when we look at words or expressions in abstraction from their situations of actual employment will hardly be resolved by a more concentrated study in the same abstraction. Instead, according to Wittgenstein, we need to see the term at work. "What *we* do is to bring words back from their metaphysical to their everyday use," he wrote.[96] The more we are reminded of the criteria for the use of a term like "understanding," and the more closely we examine the situations in which the term seems to become problematic for us, the less we may be inclined to think that there is anything which might be called "the nature of understanding."

The direction of Wittgenstein's specific remarks on "understanding" may be anticipated on the basis of this sketch of the character of his investigations. He tells us that the criteria we accept for "understanding" are considerably more complicated than we might think, and that the role and employment of the term in linguistic activity is more diverse and

more involved than we are likely to consider.[97] We are often
tempted to think of understanding as a mental state, for instance. We may speak of achieving or possessing understanding,
or perhaps of being in a state of understanding (or of comprehension). Some people have it, or are in it, while others have
not attained it. Yet "understanding" does not fit in too well
with some other things we call "mental states": depression, excitement, pain. A grammatical investigation finds some incon-
gruities here. Is understanding intermittent or episodic, like
excitement? Does it have a beginning and an end and the sort
of duration that, say, depression has? (Do we understand continuously? Or only when we are attending to something? What
happens to the understanding the rest of the time?) There appear to be more differences among these words, even among the
ones we associate with "states," than we had imagined; and the
fact that "understanding" is, grammatically, a "state" may not
be sufficient warrant for classifying it with "mental states"
generally.[98]

We may yet have the impression that understanding is something which goes on inside a person. One may "suddenly understand" something, perhaps after a period of contemplation or of
puzzling over a problem; and one may tell others when this occurs: "Now I understand." Isn't that a report on the successful completion of a process of understanding? This feature of
linguistic behavior contributes to our conviction that understanding is something that happens within, in the mind, when
the proper conditions have been met. However, the person who
"reports" thus on his understanding can be wrong about it.
After he says "Now I understand," he may go on to try out his
understanding--to finish the problem, to use the word correctly,
to make the next move--only to find out that he did not understand at all. Does that mean that he reported incorrectly
concerning his mental processes, and should go back and check
again? Or is it that he really does understand, but cannot
express or apply his understanding for some reason? We may
choose the second explanation occasionally, if, for instance,
he goes ahead to correct his mistake or to get it right the
next time. But if he consistently fails, we say (and *he* says)
that he does not understand after all. "Must I *know* when I
understand a word? Don't I also sometimes imagine myself to

understand it (as I may imagine I understand a kind of calculation) and then realize that I did not understand it?"[99]   What
makes us see whether we really understand or not (that is, what
justifies our saying that we understand) is what we go on to do.
The criteria are satisfied, or not, in our behavior. "Let us
remember," says Wittgenstein, "that there are certain criteria
in a man's behavior for the fact that he does not understand a
word: that it means nothing to him, that he can do nothing with
it. And criteria for his 'thinking he understands,' attaching
some meaning to the word, but not the right one. And, lastly,
criteria for his understanding the word right."[100] These criteria deserve more attention than they receive when we are captivated by the image of the "inner process." Wittgenstein suggests that we should regard a statement such as "Now I understand" as a signal rather than a report: its function, after
all, is not to inform us of the speaker's inner condition, but
to indicate that he is ready to go ahead, or wants no further
explanation, or wants to try again.[101] The criteria lie elsewhere.

     That "inner processes" do not come into the grammatical
situation of "understanding" is shown by another feature of our
employment of the word, which also challenges the notion that
"Now I understand" is a report. When we ask someone whether he
understands something we have just explained to him, we would
rarely be satisfied with an account of the feelings or inner
experiences he may have had while we were telling him. We
would hardly expect such a narrative in response to our question. If we want anything beyond a simple affirmative or negative reply, we want some sort of evidence that he can satisfy
the criteria we recognize: perhaps his going ahead to apply or
use whatever we have led him to understand. If he insists that
his conviction that he has performed the correct mental operations is sufficient, we may just remind him of the criteria
governing the normal employment of "understanding," and of the
distance between these criteria and his concern with an "inner
state."[102] (Under other circumstances, we might prefer to
pursue his description of his feeling or his mental activity,
to see what he does with it. But this should not be regarded
as the way to find the meaning of "understanding."[103]) "In
the sense in which there are processes (including mental pro-

cesses) which are characteristic of understanding," Wittgenstein
says, "understanding is not a mental process."[104] Even if it
could be shown that a particular feeling always accompanied certain cases of what we call "understanding," we have no warrant
to equate that feeling with the understanding.[105] It would be
better to get away from the image of the "inner process" entirely; for although various psychological processes may certainly be involved in our coming to understand something, so
that our correct use of the word "understanding" may, in a
sense, ultimately depend on these processes, we still do not
justify our use by an appeal to them. They do not figure in the
criteria for our employment of the word.[106]

Once the equation of understanding with a special inner
process has been rejected, it would be as great a mistake to
equate it with any other single activity, state, or result, as
if we had only misplaced the understanding at first and now want
to relocate it more appropriately. There is no one thing called
"understanding." There is no single defining criterion for our
use of the term either, as there might be if our use were governed by a law. The notion that our language operates according to strict rules is as misleading as the idea that every
noun stands for an object; both may be dispelled by some attention to the wide range of criteria found to operate in different situations.[107] Sometimes the criteria overlap considerably from one situation to another, but this is not inevitable,
and the common range--where it does exist--should not be taken
as putting us on the track of the "real meaning" of the term.
Always, it is the "particular circumstances" in which the word
is used which must justify our use of it.[108] If a person understands a mathematical series or a calculation, he will be
able to go ahead with it.[109] If he understands a formula or
proof, he will know how to apply it in other situations.[110]
If he claims to understand a word or expression, the criteria
may be far less definite: "We ask: How do you use the word,
what do you do with it--that will tell us how you understand
it."[111] We also speak of understanding a picture, a literary
work, a musical theme, a person--we use the term in innumerable
contexts where quite different criteria obtain.[112] And there
is no reason at all to assume that we should always be able to
formulate in words the incredibly complicated and subtle

criteria which many situations contain.[113]

There are a number of cases in which we speak of "understanding," however, when it is an ability or a capacity which is at issue. As Wittgenstein puts it, the grammar of "understands" appears to be closely related to that of "can," "is able," or "knows."[114] What we often look for is evidence of an ability, or of "mastery" of a word, a technique, or a language. ("To comprehend" and "to grasp" show a similar relationship to "mastery.") This feature of the grammar of "understanding" is evident in the first examples cited above: our claim to "understanding" will be justified, or not, by what we go on to do. If we were to insist despite all evidence against our claim that we really *do* understand (because, say, we had a flash of insight or what we would identify as an experience of comprehension), it would be clear that we were using "understanding" in some unusual way. It has become for us then what its surface grammar suggests: an experience or a state of mind brought about by a particular stimulus. But our claim that this alone is true understanding, no matter how much conviction we put into the assertion, would not ordinarily be tolerated.

Does the grammatical kinship of "understanding" and "ability" hold firm when we are discussing the understanding of religious texts and utterances? To understand what is spoken or written in general seems to have the character of a capacity or ability, for Wittgenstein. "To understand a sentence means to understand a language. To understand a language means to be master of a technique," he writes.[115] We say someone understands a sentence, or a body of utterances, when he shows that he knows what follows from it. "What we say makes a difference," as one of Wittgenstein's students observes.[116] To understand what is said, or written, is to know what difference it makes or might make: it is to know the potential employment and implications of that language in human proceedings. If we understand, we can answer correctly when some asks, "So what?" We can follow what is said--and also give an account of what follows from it.

This approach to "understanding" is already partially evident in one early assertion of Wittgenstein's. "To understand a proposition means to know what is the case if it is true."[117] It is to know "how things stand" if the proposition is true, or

to be able to say how things would be different if it were
true.[118] It is to "appreciate the range of contrast" which the
proposition opens up to us.[119] This statement comes from a
period when Wittgenstein regarded a proposition as a picture of
reality, of "what is the case." But this approach to understanding did not lose its usefulness when his view of propositions,
and of language in general, developed in other directions. To
know what follows from an utterance is still a basic criterion
of "understanding" in a great number of cases, and not only
when the utterance is a proposition.

Wittgenstein suggests looking upon language and its concepts
as instruments.[120] "Look at the sentence as an instrument,"
he said in one case, "and at its sense as its employment."[121]
If we know how to use the sentence, we understand it; or rather,
we understand it insofar as we have that ability. One obstacle
to that sort of mastery is the difficulty we have in seeing the
actual employment and functioning of language in many situations.
"A main source of our failure to understand is that we do not
command a clear view of our words. --Our grammar is lacking in
this sort of perspicuity. A perspicuous representation produces
just that understanding which consists in 'seeing connexions,'"
Wittgenstein wrote.[122] We need to be able to see how things
stand when an utterance is put into operation: how it is related to other aspects of language and behavior, what impact it
has elsewhere, or what new conditions follow from its employment.
This concept of a "perspicuous representation," according to
Wittgenstein, dominates the way we perceive and account for
things, including our linguistic behavior.[123] A clear picture
of the working of language seems to be what we need, if we are
to avoid misunderstanding. In its absence we are led *into* misunderstanding by the pictures which the surface grammar of some
expressions forces upon us.[124]

Some of the expressions and utterances we call "religious"
seem especially susceptible to misinterpretation in this respect. The pictures which a non-participant may associate with
these utterances may easily give him a false impression of
their character. If he wants to correct his impression he must
observe carefully what the "religious" person does with his
language: what conclusions he is willing to draw from his utterances, how they fit together with other statements and

activities, under what circumstances he uses certain expressions, and so on. He may then have a more accurate view of the "religious" person's pictures--that is, of how things stand when language is employed in that way. When Wittgenstein discussed religion, he stressed the difficulty of attaining an understanding of religious expressions, due at least in part from our inability to anticipate, from the surface pictures, the ways in which these expressions actually function.[125]

The various criteria for "understanding" which have been noted in the last few pages are not intended to constitute a complete description of the concept. No one of them, nor all of them together, may be taken as definitive. They are reminders. We know how to use the word well enough, ordinarily, without definition. Any effort to establish and defend a univocal mean-for the word, separating it from its instances of concrete use, must abandon grammatical inquiry and find its support else-where.[126] The advantages of a "perspicuous representation" should not commit us to the ideal of a complete picture of the use of the word, of any sort. "If I have learned to carry out a particular activity in a particular room (putting the room in order, say) and am master of this technique, it does not follow that I must be ready to describe the arrangement of the room; even if I should at once notice, and could also describe, any alteration in it," Wittgenstein writes. Similarly, a person can know his way around a city very well and still be completely incapable of drawing a map of it.[127]

The criteria for understanding an utterance seem to be closely related to those for knowing its grammar, if we compare Wittgenstein's specific remarks on "understanding" with his concept of "grammar" and with his practice of grammatical investigation. To understand an utterance, we may say, is to master its grammar.

The apparent simplicity of that remark will do no harm so long as we recall the variety of things which "mastering the grammar" may involve in any given case. As a definition of "understanding," the statement would be unacceptable. As a reminder of a range of criteria governing some of our major uses of "understanding" in connection with human utterances, it may be of some value.

Can it have any value for those concerned with the interpretation of those utterances and texts which have been called "religious"? The discussion of understanding in that context seems to have taken quite a different direction. Yet that direction has not been determined fundamentally by anything peculiarly intrinsic to religious literature, but rather by the kinds of questions which have been considered important within the general hermeneutical tradition since the early nineteenth century. A consideration of the bearing which Wittgenstein's reminders about "understanding" may have upon the concerns of that tradition, particularly as represented by Joachim Wach, may put us in a position to raise some new possibilities for the development of hermeneutics in this field.

NOTES TO CHAPTER III

1. Wach, "The Problem of Truth in Religion," p. 148; *The Comparative Study of Religions*, p. 28.

2. W. B. Gallie, *Philosophy and the Historical Understanding*, 2nd ed. (N.Y.: Schocken Books, 1968), pp. 15-16, notes an ambiguity in Dilthey's work: methodological considerations tend to merge into general reflections upon human life, history, and understanding.

3. See, e.g., Theodore Abel, "The Operation Called *Verstehen*," *Readings in the Philosophy of Science*, ed. Herbert Feigl and May Brodbeck (N.Y.: Appleton-Century-Crofts, 1953), pp. 677-687. The phrase "misplaced familiarity" is his.

4. While not necessarily central, a strong eschatological element is present in the Lotus Sutra and has figured significantly in the history of Buddhist interpretation of the Sutra. This element receives no mention in Wach's discussion of the text.

5. The relationships among these three terms--"hermeneutics," "epistemology," and "ontology"--are complex and variable. For Wach, hermeneutics is ultimately dependent upon epistemology for a model of the nature of understanding, just as epistemology depends upon metaphysics ("ontology" is rarely used) in its account of the possibility of understanding. In the wake of Heidegger, as was mentioned (p. 15 above), hermeneutics has replaced epistemology, and is both anchored in, and explicative of, ontology.

6. Karl-Otto Apel, "Das Verstehen (ein Problemgeschichte als Begriffsgeschichte)," *Archiv für Begriffsgeschichte*, I (1955), pp. 142-199, esp. pp. 198-199. Apel relies heavily on Wach in his discussion of the nineteenth-century theorists.

7. Hans-Georg Gadamer, "On the Scope and Function of Hermeneutical Reflection, "*Continuum*, VIII (1970), pp. 80, 94.

8. Richard E. Palmer, "Hermeneutics and Methodology," *Continuum*, VII (1969), p. 157.

9. *Ibid.*, p. 155.

10. Wach, *Das Verstehen*, I, p. 246, n. 1; see p. 32 above.

11. According to Palmer, no one before Gadamer has succeeded in fulfilling Schleiermacher's program and developing a "philosophically adequate and comprehensive account of understanding" (Palmer, "Hermeneutics and Methodology," pp. 155-156).

12. "Listening" is recommended by Ernst Käsemann ("Zum Thema der Urchristlichen Apokalyptik," pp. 258-259) and by Oscar Cullmann (*Salvation in History*, tr. Sidney G. Sowers [N.Y.: Harper & Row, 1967], pp. 65-74), to mention

two examples from recent theological literature; there is considerable diversity regarding the results obtained or expected.

13. Wittgenstein's life and intellectual background are discussed in G. H. von Wright's "Biographical Sketch" included in Norman Malcolm, *Ludwig Wittgenstein: A Memoir* (N.Y.: Oxford University Press, 1962), pp. 1-22, and by Stephen Toulmin, "Ludwig Wittgenstein," *Encounter*, XXXII (1969), pp. 58-71.

14. A "hermeneutical" note is heard throughout Wittgenstein's writings by, e.g., Helmut Fahrenbach, "Die logisch-hermeneutisch Problemstellung in Wittgensteins 'Tractatus,'" in *Hermeneutik und Dialektik*, II, ed. Rüdiger Bubner *et al.* (Tübingen: J. C. B. Mohr [Paul Siebeck], 1970), pp. 53-54.

15. Hans-Georg Gadamer, "Die phänomenologische Bewegung," *Philosophische Rundschau*, XI (1963), pp. 41-45.

16. Karl-Otto Apel, *Analytic Philosophy of Language and the Geisteswissenschaften*, tr. Harald Holstelilie, Foundations of Language, Supplementary Series, IV (Dordrecht: D. Reidel Publishing Company, 1967), p. 47; in Karl-Otto Apel, "Wittgenstein und das Problem des hermeneutischen Verstehens," *Zeitschrift für Theologie und Kirche*, LXIII (1966), Apel suggests that Dilthey developed the sort of meta-linguistic foundation Wittgenstein needs.

17. Walter Schulz, *Wittgenstein: Die Negation der Philosophie* (Pfullingen: Günther Neske, 1967), pp. 71-76, 112.

18. This is the hope held out by F. Kerr, "Language as Hermeneutic in the Later Wittgenstein," *Tijdschrift voor Filosofie*, XXVII (1965), pp. 519-520.

19. John M. Hems, "Husserl and-or Wittgenstein," *International Philosophical Quarterly*, VII (1968), pp. 575-578.

20. This is not to suggest that Wittgenstein cannot have known anything about the sources of the hermeneutical and phenomenological movements. Stephen Toulmin ("Ludwig Wittgenstein," pp. 70-71) suggests Wittgenstein's early acquaintance with Fritz Bühler and with the work of Eduard Spranger--both of whom, incidentally, receive appreciative notice in Wach's writings. But to connect this acquaintance with Wittgenstein's later discussion of "understanding" would require considerably more evidence.

21. When M. Gosselin, in "Enkele Beschouwingen naar Aanleiding van 'Language as Hermeneutic in the Later Wittgenstein,'" *Tijdschrift voor Filosofie*, XXVIII (1966), pp. 72-83, protests F. Kerr's Heideggerian treatment of Wittgenstein and cites several of Wittgenstein's own remarks as evidence against its accuracy, Kerr replies ("Reply to M. Gosselin," pp. 84-89 of the same volume) that she is just not willing to "put his work in the larger context" which modern interpretation demands. He does not refute her specific objections, but re-affirms the propriety of seeing Witt-

genstein's intention in a hermeneutical context, although Wittgenstein himself may not have made the necessary connections.

22. Ludwig Wittgenstein, *Philosophical Investigations*, 3rd ed., ed. G. E. M. Anscombe and Rush Rhees, tr. G. E. M. Anscombe (N.Y.: Macmillan Company, 1958). Hereafter cited as PI. Part I of this work appears substantially as it was prepared by Wittgenstein for publication. The material in Part II, together with the other posthumous publications, may be drawn upon to illuminate or extend the remarks in Part I. Following convention, Wittgenstein's writing will be cited by paragraph number with one is assigned.

23. PI, 109.

24. PI, 133.

25. PI, 109. Elsewhere he remarked parenthetically: "We want to replace wild conjectures and explanations by quiet weighing of linguistic facts" (Ludwig Wittgenstein, *Zettel*, ed. G. E. M. Anscombe and G. H. von Wright, tr. G. E. M. Anscombe [Oxford: Basil Blackwell, 1967], 447).

26. Gadamer, *Wahrheit und Methode*, pp. 483-484.

27. PI, 383.

28. PI, 25.

29. Ludwig Wittgenstein, *On Certainty*, ed. G. E. M. Anscombe and G. H. von Wright, tr. Denis Paul and G. E. M. Anscombe (Oxford: Basil Blackwell, 1969), 229; see also Wittgenstein, *Zettel*, 144, 173.

30. PI, 19, 23.

31. PI, 370.

32. Wittgenstein, *Zettel*, 444.

33. Ludwig Wittgenstein, *The Blue and Brown Books*, ed. Rush Rhees (Oxford: Basil Blackwell, 1958), pp. 17-18.

34. Ludwig Wittgenstein, *Notebooks, 1914-1916*, ed. G. H. von Wright and G. E. M. Anscombe, tr. G. E. M. Anscombe (Oxford: Basil Blackwell, 1961), pp. 48, 70. Cf. Ludwig Wittgenstein, *Tractatus Logico-Philosophicus*, tr. D. F. Pears and B. F. McGuinness (London: Routledge & Kegan Paul, 1961), 4.002.

35. Wittgenstein, *The Blue and Brown Books*, pp. 19-20. Wittgenstein occasionally spoke of this indissoluble relation of language and "the rest of our proceedings" as a "form of life." See J. F. M. Hunter, "'Forms of Life' in Wittgenstein's *Philosophical Investigations*," *American Philosophical Quarterly*, V (1968), pp. 233-243, esp. pp. 235, 241.

36. Wittgenstein, *The Blue and Brown Books*, p. 19.

37. Wittgenstein, *On Certainty*, 61.

38. PI, 43. See, e.g., George Pitcher's exposition of this passage as an "identification" of meaning and use: George Pitcher, *The Philosophy of Wittgenstein* (Englewood Cliffs, N.J.: Prentice-Hall, 1964), pp. 249-254.

39. Donald Gustafson, "On Pitcher's Account of *Investigations* 43," *Philosophy and Phenomenological Research*, XXVII (1967), pp. 252-253.

40. Ludwig Wittgenstein, *Philosophische Grammatik*, ed. Rush Rhees (Oxford: Basil Blackwell, 1969), I, 84, p. 131.

41. *Ibid.*, I, 23, p. 59. In PI, 560, he expands this comment: "I.e.: if you want to understand the use of the word 'meaning,' look for what are called 'explanations of meaning.'"

42. Wittgenstein, *On Certainty*, 601.

43. PI, 316.

44. PI, 127.

45. Wittgenstein, *Zettel*, 111.

46. Ludwig Wittgenstein, *Remarks on the Foundation of Mathematics*, ed. G. H. von Wright, Rush Rhees, and G. E. M. Anscombe, tr. G. E. M. Anscombe (Oxford: Basil Blackwell, 1964), V, 49, p. 195.

47. PI, 71.

48. PI, 107-108.

49. PI, 71, 209-210.

50. John Wisdom, "A Feature of Wittgenstein's Technique," *Paradox and Discovery* (Oxford: Basil Blackwell, 1965), p. 102.

51. Robert A. Goff, "The Wittgenstein Game," *The Christian Scholar*, XLV (1962), pp. 180-192, warns against the tendency to take the "overview statements" in the *Philosophical Investigations* as a series of summary assertions to be critically analyzed. Goff's own designation of them as "metaphors" may not be free of difficulties (Wittgenstein nowhere suggests such a view, but regards his remarks as perfectly straightforward), but the warning against bearing down on the statements as if they were empirical generalizations is appropriate.

52. E.g. PI, 90, 232, 392.

53. G. E. Moore, "Wittgenstein's Lectures in 1930-33," *Philosophical Papers* (N.Y.: Collier Books, 1962), pp. 270-271.

54. In 1929-30, Wittgenstein associated grammar more strictly with logical analysis: "Der Satz ist völlig logisch analysiert, dessen Grammatik vollkommen klargelegt ist," he wrote, and "Die Grammatik ist ein 'theory of logical types'" (Ludwig Wittgenstein, *Philosophische Bemerkungen,* ed. Rush Rhees [Oxford: Basil Blackwell, 1965], 1, p. 51 and 7, p. 54). When the ideal of complete logical analysis was renounced (see e.g. PI, 60-63), the concept of "grammar" was released from this identification and moved into greater prominence. According to Newton Garver, *Grammar and Criteria* (Ph.D. thesis, Cornell University, 1965), pp. 113-114, Wittgenstein regarded "grammar" as free from the connotations of "normative science" which "logic" carries, and hence a better term for his investigations. Garver's study gives considerable attention to Wittgenstein's "grammar" in the context of linguistics.

55. PI, 496.

56. Wittgenstein, *Philosophische Grammatik,* I, 23, p. 60. (See the editor's note, p. 487, on the date of this section.)

57. PI, p. 230.

58. PI, 353. See John Wisdom's illustrative excursus on this remark in "A Feature of Wittgenstein's Technique," pp. 98-99.

59. See Newton Garver, "Analyticity and Grammar," *The Monist,* LI (1967), p. 420; Garver, *Grammar and Criteria,* pp. 105-107.

60. Richard H. Bell, "Wittgenstein and Descriptive Theology," *Religious Studies,* V (1969), p. 17.

61. PI, 23.

62. Wittgenstein, *The Blue and Brown Books,* p. 7.

63. PI, 90.

64. PI, 664.

65. PI, 111; see Richard Bell, *Theology as Grammar: Uses of Linguistic Philosophy for the Study of Theology with Special Reference to Ludwig Wittgenstein* (Ph.D. dissertation, Yale University, 1968), pp. 103, 113, on the "depth" of language.

66. PI, 94.

67. PI, 196.

68. PI, 36: "Where our language suggests a body and there is none: there, we should like to say, is a *spirit.*"

69. PI, 104.

70. Wittgenstein, *Zettel*, 113.

71. PI, 392.

72. *Zettel*, 458.

73. PI, 572; Wittgenstein, *Zettel,* 55.

74. PI, 314.

75. Ludwig Wittgenstein, "Notes for Lectures on 'Private Experience' and 'Sense-Data,'" *Philosophical Review,* LXXVII (1968), p. 314, develops this point similarly.

76. PI, 305.

77. Wittgenstein, *Zettel*, 179.

78. PI, 77. K. T. Fann, *Wittgenstein's Conception of Philosophy* (Oxford: Basil Blackwell, 1969), pp. 43-44, suggests that Wittgenstein's experience as an elementary-school teacher (1920-26) was decisive in turning him toward a "pragmatic" view of language in his later philosophy, and is responsible for the centrality of "learning" and "use" as keys to understanding language in that later thought.

79. PI, 572.

80. PI, 355.

81. Rogers Albritton, "On Wittgenstein's Use of the Term 'Criterion,'" *Wittgenstein: The Philosophical Investigations,* ed. George Pitcher (Garden City, N.Y.: Doubleday & Company, Anchor Books, 1966), pp. 243-244.

82. PI, 580.

83. Wittgenstein, *Philosophische Grammatik*, I, 43, p. 87.

84. H. R. Smart, "Language-Games," *Philosophical Quarterly,* VII (1957), p. 232.

85. Ernst Konrad Specht, *The Foundations of Wittgenstein's Late Philosophy*, tr. D. E. Walford (Manchester: Manchester University Press, 1969), p. 25.

86. *Ibid.*, p. 97.

87. Moore, "Wittgenstein's Lectures in 1930-33," pp. 253-254.

88. PI, 132.

89. See Newton Garver, "Wittgenstein on Criteria," *Knowledge and Experience*, ed. C. D. Rollins (Pittsburgh: University of Pittsburgh Press, 1962), pp. 62-63.

90. Wittgenstein, *On Certainty*, 559.

91. Philip Hallie, "Wittgenstein's Grammatical-Empirical Distinction," *Journal of Philosophy*, LX (1963), pp. 575-578, says that Wittgenstein's refusal to provide a "detailed doctrine" concerning the empirical foundations of grammatical conventions forces us ("by his own default") to accept a negative account. Perhaps it would be better to resist the compulsion to have a doctrine.

92. PI, 124.

93. PI, 241.

94. E.g., PI, 58, 116.

95. The differences between this sort of "agreement" and the hermeneutical concept of "pre-understanding" will be explored further in the next chapter.

96. PI, 116; see also 38.

97. PI, 182.

98. PI, 59; see also 146, 148.

99. PI, p. 53. The outward evidence is generally convincing even for the speaker; and he does not regard it as an error in his reporting, but as a misunderstanding or a failure to understand. See K. W. Rankin, "Wittgenstein on Meaning, Understanding, and Intending," *American Philosophical Quarterly*, III (1966), p. 7.

100. PI, 269.

101. PI, 180.

102. PI, p. 181; Wittgenstein, *Zettel*, 193.

103. The grammar of his assertion has not yet been made clear to us, we might say; cf. Wittgenstein, *The Blue and Brown Books*, p. 10, for a case with some similarities to this one.

104. PI, 154.

105. PI, 153; p. 181.

106. Cf. Wittgenstein's remarks on the "psychological process" view in Friedrich Waismann, *Wittgenstein und der Wiener Kreis*, ed. B. F. McGuinness (Oxford: Basil Blackwell, 1967), pp. 167-168.

107. Wittgenstein, *The Blue and Brown Books*, pp. 23-28; PI, 77-84. John W. Cook, "Human Beings," *Studies in the Philosophy of Wittgenstein*, ed. Peter Winch (London: Routledge & Kegan Paul, 1969), pp. 133-140, stresses the fact that Wittgenstein's use of "criteria" is directed not only against the tyranny of "inner processes" but also, and more fundamentally, against the tendency to search for a common element or a single defining criterion in all our uses of a term.

108. PI, 154-155.

109. PI, 151-155.

110. Wittgenstein, *Remarks on the Foundations of Mathematics,*
IV, 25, p. 146.

111. Wittgenstein, *Philosophische Grammatik,* I, 43, p. 87.

112. PI, 526-533.

113. PI, 78.

114. PI, 150.

115. PI, 199.

116. Rush Rhees, "Can There Be a Private Language?", *Discussions of Wittgenstein* (London: Routledge & Kegan Paul,
1970), p. 55.

117. Wittgenstein, *Tractatus Logico-Philosophicus,* 4.024.

118. Wittgenstein, *Notebooks, 1914-1916,* p. 18.

119. The phraise is from Dennis O'Brien, "The Unity of Wittgenstein's Thought," *Ludwig Wittgenstein: The Man and his
Philosophy,* ed. K. T. Fann (N.Y.: Dell Publishing Co.,
1967), pp. 403-404.

120. PI, 569.

121. PI, 421.

122. PI, 122.

123. In Ludwig Wittgenstein, "Bemerkungen über Frazers *The
Golden Bough*," *Synthese,* XVII (1967), p. 241, he wonders
if this is not a *Weltanschauung,* typical for our time.
Cf. PI, 122.

124. PI, 422-427.

125. Ludwig Wittgenstein, *Lectures and Conversations on
Aesthetics, Psychology,and Religious Belief,* compiled from
notes taken by Yorick Smythies, Rush Rhees, and James
Taylor, ed. Cyril Barrett (Berkeley and Los Angeles:
University of California Press, 1967), pp. 53-72, esp.
pp. 62, 71-72.

126. Wittgenstein, *The Blue and Brown Books,* pp. 27-28.

127. Wittgenstein, *Zettel,* 120.

The Requirements of Hermeneutics

Despite the apparent ease with which recent hermeneutical writers can assimilate some features of Wittgenstein's philosophy to their own mode of thought and to the hermeneutical tradition generally, a clear contrast between the two ways of dealing with "understanding" is evident. For Wittgenstein, "understanding" is a word which may be appropriately employed in a great variety of circumstances; it is not the name of a particular process or event, a "happening"--as Gadamer puts it --precipitated under certain conditions when man interacts with his world.[1] The image of an inner event or process is from Wittgenstein's viewpoint a misconception, encouraged by the superficial grammar of the term "understanding" and of some of the expressions in which it occurs. He points to a selection of the diverse criteria governing the use of the word as evidence against any claim that it has a single meaning or referent.

But from the hermeneutician's standpoint, it is this diversity of use which is superficial, while the unity of understanding is fundamental. Understanding may have different forms under different conditions, but a deeper inquiry will reveal an underlying phenomenon of which these are only different levels or dimensions. Wach's recognition of various degrees of understanding culminating in "integral comprehension" is one illustration of this; Gadamer's intention to "search out that which is common to all forms of understanding" is another.[2] In either case, the diversity of use to which Wittgenstein would draw our attention must be made to yield to a more fundamental unity: the event of understanding. Wach defends his conception of the process of understanding by anchoring it in metaphysical principles which he believes are at least implicitly acknowledged by every successful interpreter. Gadamer unfolds the concept of understanding directly into an ontological schema which then serves as the context for all further particular interpretation. Though their methods of defending (or explicating) the unity of understanding differ, these hermeneuticians agree in regarding understanding as something or some "happening" whose nature can be more or less clearly delimited and discussed.

Some of the problems which follow upon the acceptance of such a view of understanding have already been suggested. If the goal of an interpretative effort is said to be understanding, and if we believe understanding to be a particular state, experience, or process, then we may be inclined to be interested in the text only insofar as it may contribute to the realization of whatever we believe understanding to be. The text becomes an instrument for our use. Through it we may recapitulate the author's inner experience, or achieve a re-cognition of that aspect of the human spirit which he was trying to express, or simply deepen our own self-understanding—the goal, in any case, will depend on our image of the nature of the basic phenomenon called "understanding."

This centrality of the reader's image of understanding in any interpretative situation was explicitly acknowledged and positively affirmed by Rudolf Bultmann. He portrayed this theme as a consistent development of Dilthey's emphasis on the interpreter's *Interesse*.[3] Bultmann was careful to stress that the reader is not at liberty simply to make of the text whatever he wishes: the possibilities are limited by the nature of the text. The idea of the necessity of a correlation between the reader's interest and preparation, on the one side, and the possibilities residing in the text, on the other, was shared by Wach. And because of his recognitive model of understanding, Wach saw the possibility of such a correlation as the basis for objectivity in understanding. The text *is* an instrument, through which the author's inner experience is communicated to the reader. That experience is the ultimate meaning of the text, accessible only through the process of understanding. So understanding can be said to be objective; it involves no fanciful conjecture, reductionism, distortion, or misuse of the text, but reveals the very heart of its meaning.

But how can this claim to objectivity be justified? In

order for it to stand, it must already be established that the nature of the text is such that its ultimate meaning is accessible to us in understanding. Wach accordingly explains the accessibility of the texts with which he is concerned by saying that they are all fundamentally expressions of religious experience, which is an aspect of the universal human *a priori*. But a text can be identified as "religious" only on the basis of a prior, anticipatory grasp of its nature. The meaning of a text, then, is that which is revealed through the process of understanding; we are justified in claiming objectivity for this process because we know the nature of the text; and we know the nature of the text because we already understand its essential meaning. There is an inescapable circularity, which Wach prefers to consider benign, rather than vicious, in the process of understanding; it corresponds to his conception of the hermeneutical circle.

This circularity imprints itself upon the language of hermeneutics. Key terms in Wach's discussion are defined in terms of one another, as we have just seen, and all are related to his idea of what goes on within a person when he understands something. That idea dominates the discussion and largely shapes the definition not only of such terms as "meaning" and "objectivity," but also of the interpreter's task and goal generally. The grammar of hermeneutics, we might say, is bound to the image of understanding.

But why should it be? Is it simply that Wach, and the hermeneutical writers generally, are so captivated by the surface grammar of "understanding" that they are driven to ask about the nature of understanding rather than being content to study the use of the word? This conclusion is tempting. We might view hermeneutics as it has developed since Schleiermacher as a "disease of language." Taking pity on its sufferers, we could prescribe a regimen of grammatical investigation to cure them of these pathological notions. Such a course might draw support from some of Wittgenstein's remarks on philosophy: he said, "The philosopher's treatment of a question is like the treatment of an illness," and he compared the methods of philosophy to "different therapies."[4] Some of his suggestions concerning the reasons for our susceptibility to linguistic illness have already been mentioned, e.g. our "craving for generality" and our

readiness to seize the surface grammar of an expression and to
posit a substance behind every abstract noun. If this seems to
offer a plausible explanation for the development of hermeneutics in its present form, perhaps these thinkers need to be reminded of the conventional grammar of "understanding" and of
other words in the hermeneutical vocabulary, and persuaded to
renounce an unprofitable line of inquiry.

The temptation to treat hermeneutics in this way may be
strong, but some other considerations may help us decide to resist it. First, Wittgenstein does not offer his remarks on the
origins of our linguistic difficulties as either accusations or
explanatory hypotheses. He writes in a confessional mode, as
Stanley Cavell has indicated.[5] The tendencies he condemns are
his own. He confesses his own fascination with the superficial
"pictures," his own temptation to take language the wrong way.
These observations are not sweeping charges concerning the
sources of philosophical difficulty. As such, they would require considerably more theoretical elaboration and factual
backing than he ever provides. Nor are the specific reminders
he suggests panaceas to dissolve all conceptual problems. They
are oriented toward the real needs evident in particular cases.
Other people may find that they share the same difficulty; they
may join in Wittgenstein's confession and benefit from his reminders. But to take a confessional statement as a hypothesis,
and to impose a particular reminder upon a situation as a general solution, is to take liberties with the material.

Secondly, there is no sign that the hermeneuticians would
be likely to receive Wittgenstein's grammatical remarks as a
genuine contribution to the discussion in which they are involved. As some of their statements already cited indicate,
they may be willing to incorporate some features of Wittgenstein's philosophy into their discussion on another level; but
the distance between ontology or phenomenology on the one hand,
and observations about grammar on the other, seems so obviously
great that the latter can have no serious relevance to the
problems generated in the former. Rather than being persuaded
to abandon his method of inquiry, the hermeneutician confronted
by a list of grammatical observations might be more inclined to
retort that they are simply not helpful; they do not address
his problem. It is not that there is anything wrong with them.

As remarks about the ordinary use of language they may be un-
exceptionable. "But," as one critic of Wittgenstein has asked,
"of what possible philosophical interest or importance could a
question like this be--a question about how we ordinarily use
the word 'understand'? We all learned how to use this and many
other words successfully early in life. Wittgenstein's answer
is true, but trivial. This, of course, is what Wittgenstein
often said himself about his discoveries. But if they are trivial, why are they important? It would seem that they cannot
really be both."[6] Wittgenstein, he concludes, cannot seriously
be regarded as offering an alternative to a thoroughgoing investigation of the nature of understanding. It is dangerous,
in fact, to think that anything important could be settled by
Wittgenstein's investigations.[7] Another opponent (whose representation of Wittgenstein's work as a caricature of phenomenology
has already been mentioned) remarks sarcastically: "We no longer
have to examine ourselves (a tiresome and occasionally embarrass-
ing business), we are not interested in how human consciousness
works, only in how *verbs* work!"[8]

According to Wittgenstein, a difficulty characteristic of
philosophical investigation is that of recognizing a solution
as a solution once it is found. If the form of our inquiry
makes it look as though an explanation of something were required, while the real solution is a description, we may treat
the description as a preliminary (if not simply trivial) statement and go on in search of something more substantial. What
we need to do, says Wittgenstein, is to give the description
"the right place in our considerations," to dwell upon it until
its full contribution as a solution is realized. He says, "The
difficulty here is: to stop."[9] It may be necessary to transform
the investigation before the solution can be appreciated. This
does not mean dropping one sort of question because it is too
difficult and finding a new question to fit the answer at hand.
It may mean trading one formulation of the problem for another,
restating the issue so that the actual problem is brought more
fully to light. We run into trouble when a problem is so closely
bound up in our thinking with a particular statement of it that
we can no longer envision an alternative statement. The problem itself is obscured, and subsidiary problems, perhaps oc-
casioned by the form of the statement, may dominate the dis-

cussion and take it far from its origin. At such a time, we need to rediscover the problem with which we began and to redirect the investigation in accordance with what is really at issue.[10] This is no simple assignment, and we cannot assume that the application of a certain method, like a few drops of a chemical reagent, will automatically reveal the underlying problem. In an early note--long before the idea of "grammatical investigation" was expressed--Wittgenstein said, "One of the most difficult of the philosopher's task is to find out where the shoe pinches."[11] Its difficulty became increasingly apparent to Wittgenstein himself, as he moved from general philosophical solutions to more and more specific and sensitive explorations of individual problems.

Just as it is possible to fail to recognize a solution, and to go on without stopping to consider what may appear obvious and inconsequential, one may sometimes stop too soon. A solution may be imposed on a problem before the requirements of the problem have been fully assessed; and in that case the difficulties are bound to return, at some time, perhaps in another form. In his recent contribution to literary hermeneutics, *Validity in Interpretation*, E. D. Hirsch draws upon Wittgenstein's work in an attempt to separate hermeneutics from the imagery of mental processes, in its treatment of both "meaning" and "understanding." "Meaning" does not reside in words, he finds, nor in some "magic land" apart from human consciousness and activity.[12] But it is not to be identified in "psychologistic" fashion with a private meaning-experience, either. "Meaning experiences *are* private, but they are not meanings."[13] Understanding, therefore, does not involve finding some special access to the writer's private experiences and sharing them. There is no such immediacy, in any case.[14] To be sure, understanding begins with a *guess*--an imaginative, "unmethodical, intuitive, sympathetic" preliminary conjecture as to the meaning; this corresponds to what has traditionally been called the "divinatory moment." But it is no more than a guess: it carries no certainty, but is only the point at which the work of understanding starts.[15] Understanding is the critical, indispensable task of testing the original conjecture against all relevant information and refining it, meanwhile developing its field of implications. "Most of the practical problems of

interpretation are problems of implication," according to
Hirsch.[16] No meaning is manifest; it must always be construed.
Hermeneutics should be concerned with the establishment of the
principles by which valid implications may be drawn, rather
than with the attempt to find a method by which we might reconstruct something in the author's psyche. "The discipline of
interpretation is founded, then, not on a methodology of construction but on a logic of validation."[17] The hypothetical
moment in understanding must always be followed by the critical,
and it is with the latter, rather than (as has traditionally
been the case) with the former, that hermeneutics should be
occupied.[18]

Hirsch shares with Wittgenstein and others a conviction
not only that "meaning" and "understanding" should not be identified with mental processes (Gadamer, as Hirsch notes, also
rejects that particular equation), but that any claim to understanding must be justified by outward, public criteria.[19] The
meaning of a text is constant, determined by the author's will;
the interpreter must do justice to it by drawing the correct
implications, i.e. by knowing what follows from the statements
of the text and what does not. The interpreter is bound to
the authorial will so long as he seeks valid understanding.
He may not simply subject the text to the demands of whatever
he considers "understanding" to be, but must subject his understanding to criticism.[20] He may do what he wishes in the
way of evaluation or response afterward. He is independent of
the authorial will after the meaning has been correctly construed.

Hirsch's desire to concentrate on the aspect of validation, as a corrective to the usual hermeneutical preoccupation
with what he regards as the preliminary matter, reflects his
judgment as to the location of the key questions in hermeneutics. They center for him on the issue of settling disputes
in interpretation--of validating or discounting an interpreter's
claims to understand. These questions are not to be answered
by referring to the process by which the original guesses or
hypotheses are conceived. Thus far, Hirsch would seem to be
contributing to the liberation of the object of understanding
from any given image of the process of understanding.

But his emphasis on valid implication as the test of

understanding raises for him another sort of question, which
reinstates to some extent the epistemological orientation of
traditional hermeneutics: How is implication possible? As
Hirsch portrays it, the divinatory guessing with which the interpreter begins may be unmethodical, but it is not random.
And after a guess has been made, the process of drawing implications has a sort of logic to it (though it is not to be
equated with logical implication); we do not offer an endless
series of wild conjectures and wait to be told whether we have
happened to hit upon some correct implications. We know,
roughly, what implications follow in any given case, and if we
find our attempts refuted, we decide that our original hypothesis was incorrect and we try again. If our guess is correct, we will be able to draw the correct implications.[21]
Valid understanding therefore depends upon making the right
move, settling upon the right idea, in the "divinatory moment."
Hirsch leaves the realm of "inner processes" in his definition
of understanding, only to be drawn back into it when he finds
it necessary to explain the conditions of valid implication--
that is, the conditions of understanding.

Hirsch relies upon a concept of *types* in his treatment of
this theme. A type is an idea in the consciousness of a writer
or reader. It can be expressed in linguistic symbols and thus
communicated to another; the meaning of an utterance is determined by the type-idea which the utterer wishes to share. In
Hirsch's terminology, "a verbal meaning is a willed type."[22]
In order to understand the meaning encountered in a text, a
reader must recognize the type; and for this he must already
possess the type, at least in a general form, in his own consciousness. Since there is no immediacy in understanding, the
reader cannot share the author's idea by any sort of intuition.
But the type in one person's mind may be identical with that
in another person's mind, and on this identity understanding
rests.[23] The guess with which understanding begins is an attempt to match types correctly. That guess may be directed
by an "anticipated sense of the whole," the consciousness of
the type which is already possessed--the equivalent, for
Hirsch, of the traditional "pre-understanding" (*Vorverständ-
nis*).[24] All understanding depends on pre-understanding, for
"if the type were not shared by the interpreter, he could not

draw implications."[25] We can know what a particular meaning involves only because we already know its type.

Hirsch acknowledges his theory of types to be a form of the hermeneutical circle, and thinks that Dilthey's idea that (as Hirsch puts it) "an individual entity can be known only through a type" is inescapable. The pre-understood type not only introduces us to the object, but also *constitutes* it for us to some degree, governing our perception of it and dominating particularly where the objective meaning is not entirely explicit to us.[26] We fill in the obscure portions on the basis of our preconception, since we are familiar with the type. Hirsch's reference to Dilthey at this point makes even more apparent the similarity of his account of how understanding occurs to that represented by Wach, despite divergences at several places. Central to both is the image of recognition as the key element from which all else follows. Once the type, idea, or aspect of experience embodied in the text is identified and "placed" in the interpreter's consciousness, everything in the text and everything which follows from the text may be organized around that focal point. The "meaning" is something which is expressed in the language of the text, and which is to be retrieved and reconstituted or re-experienced by the reader. This is impossible unless the reader already possesses the pattern. Whether it is a learned type (as for Hirsch[27]) or a cultivated, latent "sense" for the object (as for Wach), its role in the account of understanding is the same: it tends to become the focus, determining what can be understood and governing the way in which it is understood. An epistemological investigation of the foundations or origins of the pre-understanding may be deferred (as it is by both Wach and Hirsch), but the propriety and ultimate necessity of such an investigation is acknowledged.[28]

Hirsch's goals are not unlike Wach's. He wants to preserve the possibility of objective understanding--that is, of reproducing the meaning as determined by the author--against various claims that such objectivity is impossible or that it is not true understanding.[29] He bases the idea that objectivity belongs with understanding on the fact that any claim to valid understanding must subject itself to the ordinary criteria for the evaluation of such a claim, and "the only compelling normative principle that has ever been brought forward is the old-fashioned ideal of rightly understanding what the author meant."[30] This brings understanding out into the open, involving the interpreter in the work of drawing valid implications to satisfy the public criteria of understanding. These aspects of Hirsch's treatment seem to correspond most closely to ideas which might be derived from Wittgenstein: the reliance on ordinary criteria both for the meaning of "understanding" and for the validation of particular claims to undersatnd. But then Hirsch finds it necessary to return to a consideration of the process of understanding and the phenomenon of recognition, and to appeal to a theory of types, in order to explain and defend the *possibility* of the sort of understanding he seeks. Here he is once again in the company of Dilthey and Wach, having decided that Wittgenstein can offer no help with this dimension of the inquiry.[31] Its form has already been determined in a mode more congenial to the language and patterns of response of the traditional hermeneutical figures. The question has been set, we might say, by those Hirsch wants to oppose: by the advocates of "psychologistic" and "radical historicist" views of understanding.[32] He perceives their refusal to associate understanding with objectivity as a challenge which requires a defense in the same terms; and so, like Betti (whose influence upon Hirsch is both acknowledged and evident), he attempts to vindicate Dilthey's position in certain respects without becoming enmeshed in the network of philosophical threads which support its concepts of "type" and of "objectivity."

If Hirsch's use of Wittgenstein is any indication, perhaps we may not expect that Wittgenstein's work will be of any more assistance to us when it brought into contact with hermeneutics than the hermeneutical writers already cited are willing to admit when they put his writings into their context. But it is more likely that Hirsch's work does not represent (nor did he intend to undertake) the most thorough examination of the hermeneutical questions which would be possible in the light of Wittgenstein's discussion of "understanding." Hirsch cites Wittgenstein mainly in support of his concept of "genre" or "type" as systems of conventions by which the use of language is governed; but even here Wittgenstein's usefulness to him is limited, and he finds it necessary to go beyond these observations to give the "type-experiences" a theoretical foundation.

He applies some of Wittgenstein's ideas to problems whose terms
have already been established, and when the procedure leaves
some questions unanswered he returns to the hermeneutical tradition to carry the discussion further.

Hirsch's use of Wittgenstein has been stressed in the last
few pages; a thorough appreciation and criticism of his book
would have to involve the consideration of many other features
of its content and purposes. Its importance for us is in illustrating that, even when it is acknowledged that the meaning
of "understanding" and the adequacy of any particular understanding are questions to be settled by referring to the various
criteria governing the use of language (and not by examining an
inner process or an event called "understanding"), all hermeneutical issues have not thereby been laid to rest. The problem of the *conditions* of understanding is particularly prominent.
It appears, in the terms in which it is usually cast, to be an
epistemological question requiring an epistemological response;
and the response given tends to color the remainder of the hermeneutical treatment, even when the inquiry into the inner process of understanding has previously been rejected as misleading. A closer examination of the circumstances in which this
apparently epistemological problem develops might suggest an
alternate approach to it which would not lead inexorably back
into the traditional setting of the problem, with its circularity.

The importance of the question of the conditions of understanding is evident from the central position and extensive
treatment it receives in Wach's account of hermeneutics. According to Wach, two related questions dominate the history of
hermeneutical reflection: the first is that of the nature of
understanding, and the second is that of its conditions, both
empirical and *a priori*.[33] In response to the first, Wach believes, an ideal of understanding must be established and defended against any admixture of evaluation, explanation, "decision," or application. An unambiguous definition and defense
of true understanding is necessary in order to settle the conflicting claims which arise when various, frequently mutually
exclusive methods of interpretation are applied to a text.
If a unified description of understanding can be founded upon
universal valid principles, a standard can be imposed upon the

prevailing chaos. Interpreters will be constrained to demonstrate the adequacy of their claims in the light of the general
norms of understanding, or to modify their claims and admit
that genuine understanding is not their primary interest.

The second question, arising out of the same circumstances,
is very closely related to the first. This kinship has encouraged a tendency to see the second question simply as an aspect
of the first. For example, when particular conditions have
been imposed upon understanding--assent, faith, or the acceptance and application of certain normative canons of interpre-
tation--these conditions seem to merge with the definition of
understanding itself, and indeed to function as criteria for
"understanding." "You cannot understand unless you believe"
has the appearance of an assertion which might be subject to a
test of verification, say, by examining an unbeliever who claims
to understand to see whether his claim is warranted. But it can
also be taken as a criterion for "understanding": that is, anyone who does not believe *cannot be said* to understand, because
understanding, in this usage, implies belief. This second
function appears to prevail in some exclusivist accounts of
understanding, in which it is axiomatic that any "true" or
"full" comprehension is reserved to insiders--however that
status is to be determined. Here, conditions of understanding
are established by definition rather than by investigation.

Even if this somewhat arbitrary way of handling the issue
is repudiated, the sort of inquiry which is appropriate as a
basis for a response to the question of the conditions of understanding is not clear. The ambiguity here is to some extent
only a reflection and consequence of that which we have already
seen in the prior question about understanding itself. Is it a
question about understanding or about "understanding"--the nature of a phenomenon or the use of a word? The fact that it
has generally been pursued as if it were a question of the
first sort should not obscure its grammatical dimension entirely. One purpose of the hermeneutical inquiry, as envisioned
by Schleiermacher, was to settle disputes about the use of
"understanding." What counts as "understanding"? When is a
person justified in saying that he understands? How can some
generally acceptable criteria or standards be set? Ordinary
criteria for the use of "understanding" were often being

supplanted by special criteria, such as the *a priori* conditions
just mentioned, when the interpretation of Scripture was being
considered. To the advocate of "general hermeneutics," this
imposition of special requirements constituted a misuse of "understanding": the Bible is to be understood in the same way as
any other book. That is, although we must pay attention to its
particularity, as with any distinct form of literature, the criteria for "understanding" with regard to the Bible cannot be
wholly different from those which apply in other cases. (In
Schleiermacher's terms, the special must be related to the general. Otherwise we have only an aggregate of unrelated rules
and requirements which "come into collision."[34]) There must be
some consistency and coherence in our use of words. It was to
facilitate this that Schleiermacher wanted to get back to the
"simple fact of understanding," before it is overlaid with special definitions and conditions, and to recover here a meaning
which might be recognized by all and invoked as a standard.[35]

An attempt at such a recovery of the primordial phenomenon
of understanding must include, as Wach later emphasized, a
clarification of the conditions of understanding. The proper
clarification would not only eliminate the various special conditions wrongly imposed as criteria, but also establish a basis
for a constructive statement: What does valid understanding
really presuppose? Thus phrased, the question still admits of
a range of possible modes of investigation.[36] Thus, when the
attempt to deal with the question, "What is understanding?",
began to develop as an investigation of the nature of the process of understanding, the problem of the conditions of understanding also took on an epistemological cast. Rather than
being treated as an empirical question—"Under what conditions,
in what circumstances, is understanding acquired?" or "How does
one get into a position to satisfy the criteria for 'understanding'?"—it was perceived as an epistemological one: "What
are the (transcendental) conditions of the possibility of understanding?" or more simply, "How is understanding possible?" The
answer to this question is to be developed in the explication of
the nature of the understanding-event itself.

Although this epistemological orientation is decisive for
Wach's treatment of the issue of the conditions of understanding, it does not exhaust his concern with that issue. Wach was

not willing to allow hermeneutics to be transformed into epistemology (or psychology), as we have already seen. He was sensitive to the distinctive character of the *hermeneutical* questions about understanding, imparted by the circumstances of their origin. The hermeneutical inquiry is not motivated by curiosity about the workings of the human mind, but rather by a practical need to discover and establish a goal or ideal, a criterion, for the interpretation of texts, and to point the way to its attainment. Hermeneutics is concerned with the understanding of texts; and the understanding of understanding is important only insofar as it may contribute to that prior concern. Though hermeneutics should not consist simply of practical advice or rules of procedure, its ultimate aim is the facilitation of understanding; and, for Wach, understanding implies an object.

Schleiermacher's objection to a hermeneutics consisting only of unrelated rules was not that it was practical rather than theoretical, but that it led, in practice, to incoherence, superficiality, and misunderstanding which might be avoided if hermeneutics were a little less immediately "practical" and a little more reflective. Wach recognized this practical orientation, and directed his treatment of the conditions of understanding accordingly, when he refused to linger over the epistemological dimension of the question as such but instead related his account of the *a priori* conditions of understanding to the specific problem of the interpreter's preparation: the necessity of cultivating the "sense for religion," for example, along with the ability to balance the *a priori* element with the various empirical components of the interpretative effort.

In carrying the discussion of the conditions of understanding beyond the general epistemological realm, and seeking some specification of the conditions to be met in a particular realm of interpretation, Wach was following Dilthey's methodological principles as well as what he took to be Schleiermacher's ultimately practical intention. He recalled Dilthey's description of hermeneutics as the "connecting link" between the concerns of philosophy generally and the concern of each particular discipline to interpret its material correctly; and he shared Dilthey's conviction that the requirements of understanding cannot be determined in abstraction from these indi-

vidual disciplines. We might say that, for Wach, philosophy
may uncover the formal conditions of understanding, as they are
derived from the fundamental nature of understanding itself,
while the material conditions are dictated by the nature of the
material to be understood. Wach concentrated on the material
conditions for understanding religious texts: the character of
the text as an expression of religious experience, and the corresponding presence in the interpreter of a developed sensitivity to religious expression. He assumed the formal conditions
implicit in the image of understanding as a recognitive process:
the existence of some prior principle of identity between subject and object which can be brought to consciousness in concrete form through the interpreter's experience with the text.

The conditions which accompany the general image of understanding which Wach accepts naturally set the terms within which
the material conditions for a specific realm of interpretation
may be elaborated, and dominate the description of the interpreter's task. We saw how Wach's illustrative interpretation
of the Lotus Sutra was shaped by the need to find a universal,
a point of correspondence between text and reader. In the interpreter's preparation, nothing is so important as the sharp-
ening of a sensitivity to the general form of religious experience presumed to be embodied in the text. This enables the
reader to separate the internal and essential from the accidental circumstances of its expression in language. Little else
in the way of preparation is required. A sensitive reader is
able not only to recognize the basic "religiosity" of the Sutra,
but, upon careful and sympathetic reading, to discern more specifically the type of religious experience expressed and to
grasp the spirit, the individual character, imparted to the
text through the striving of this experience for adequate expression. All this constitutes understanding.

If Wach's account of interpretation is found deficient in
its treatment of operational method, perhaps it is because his
picture of understanding leads him to locate the crucial operations "within" the reader. Of course, the interpreter must
know enough about the linguistic and cultural context and historical circumstances of the text to overcome its initial
strangeness and to gauge the extent of external influence upon
its development. But this external, "objective" preparation is

all preliminary or auxiliary to the real occurrence of understanding: it facilitates understanding, and a valid interpretation cannot contradict the facts which have been objectively
established. But it is not yet a part of understanding, in-
gredient in the process as is the "sense for religion." Consequently, this empirical aspect of the conditions of understanding does not receive the same attention from Wach as those
inner conditions which are more closely tied, in his view, to
the actual process, the "happening," of understanding.

There is a significant gap between the mechanics of interpretation, as stressed by the grammatical-historical school and
its successors, and the primordial phenomenon of the intuitive
grasp of meaning which is the keystone of integral comprehension. The roots of this division are deep.[37] It was inherited
by the nineteenth-century theorists, whose history Wach traced
just by examining the various ways in which the division was
successively treated. If either element were to be given free
rein, with the other held in check, the results would be disas-
trous. For Wach, massive grammatical-historical knowledge
about a text does not necessarily lead to comprehension; the
result might instead be a meaningless catalogue of facts, isolated bits of information. But "intuition" can also be decep-
tive, and an interpretation based solely on the inner dimension
without external checks is generally unreliable, though it may
be powerfully convincing. Further, the exalting of the intuitive element leads to an anarchistic or antinomian situation
in which every interpreter is left with his own impressions.

From Wach's viewpoint, then, hermeneutics was faced with
the task of finding and maintaining a balance between the objective and subjective elements in the act of understanding.
As Schleiermacher had envisioned the goal, the two dimensions
should be in such harmony that each exactly confirms the results of the other. Neither dimension is subordinate to the
other, properly speaking. Under ideal conditions, each should
be able to supplant the other and duplicate its results.[38]

That ideal of the mutual criticism and confirmation of
the two dimensions is continued in Wach's theme of "integral
comprehension," in which each component of interpretation
blends with, reinforces, and extends the whole. But it is
extremely difficult to specify the terms of the relationship

between the elements so as to throw light on the procedure to
be followed by an interpreter who seeks the proper balance or
integration of components. Or rather, the more closely the relationship is specified by Wach, the more evident it becomes
that the sort of reciprocity envisioned by Schleiermacher cannot be realized, at least as Wach develops the hermeneutical
situation. The objective and subjective dimensions do not and
cannot yield interchangeable results. Each contributes something vital to the total task of understanding, but their contributions are of entirely different kinds and neither can
duplicate the function or the results of the other. Objective
investigation provides a foundation for the act of understanding, and sets some limits to its possibilities: what is objectively established may not be contradicted by subjective insight.
The understanding must operate within the framework given by empirical, grammatical-historical knowledge of the text. But the
provision of such a framework is the extent of the contribution
which the objective dimension may make to understanding. The
actual discovery and comprehension of the meaning of the text--
that is, the event of understanding itself--is reserved to the
a priori dimension. The meaning cannot be developed or produced;
it can only be recognized. To be sure, the interpreter's perception of the meaning can be sharpened and corrected by referring again to the empirical data and the possibilities it allows, and there is a reciprocal movement between the subjective
and objective realms as the meaning is critically refined and
the details of the text are illuminated and related to its
central spirit. But the initiative rests with the *a priori* dimension, and, so long as the bounds of the empirical are not
transgressed, everything depends upon that inner process of
grasping and recognizing the meaning. That, essentially, is
understanding.

Given the crucial importance of the inner process, and
its odd distance from the empirical study of the text, it is
not remarkable that Wach should devote his attention to the
investigation of its nature and conditions, and that his treatment should have so little bearing on operational method. There
is nothing problematical about the methods or the aims of the
objective study of texts, for Wach. Such study is ·preparatory:
it opens up a text so that its meaning may be extracted,

examined, and related to its context, in understanding. What is
problematical is the hidden, spontaneous process of understanding itself, and what it requires of both text and interpreter.
And therefore Wach directs his efforts toward the description
of the transcendental conditions of the possibility of understanding religious texts.

Some of the versatility of the term "understanding" is felt
by the hermeneutical theorist when he finds, in trying to give a
coherent account of its meaning, that he must nevertheless deal
with it under two aspects. The hermeneutical treatment of understanding under the two headings of its nature and its conditions reflects a duality which is already present in ordinary,
non-technical use of the term. The question, "What is understanding?" may be a request for a definition: "What do we call
'understanding'?" of "What counts as 'understanding'?" A description of a "state" might satisfy the inquirer. But the question might also be taken as one about the *way* to this state: "How
can one come to understand?" or "How does understanding work?"
What is wanted is some account of the realization or achievement
of the state of understanding. This duality reinforces the tendency to treat "understanding" as the name of a mysterious inner
phenomenon, since this image--comprising both "state" and "process"--serves as a ready vehicle for the visualization of understanding.

If we accept that image as a vehicle also for a more strict
and technical treatment of understanding, as do the theorists
represented by Wach, we may first try to characterize the basic
nature of understanding, isolating and describing the proto-
phenomenon at the heart of all particular instances of understanding. Then we may attempt to determine the conditions which
permit that phenomenon to appear, given the basic conception of
it which we have formulated. Here, we find ourselves asking on
the one hand what it is about the object of understanding--say,
a religious text--which renders it comprehensible; and on the
other hand what it is about the interpreter which enables him to
understand it. In Wach's case, an answer to the first question
involves the specification of the locus of meaning of a text:
the meaning is the experience which the text embodies as "objective spirit" and expresses to the receptive reader. This

answer rests in turn upon assumptions about the nature of religion and the nature and function of language. The second question leads him to a theory of the religious *a priori*, the innate capacity to re-cognize religious experience in its expressions. This, too, involves theoretical assumptions about religion and language, and requires in addition some minimal philosophical-psychological account of human nature, as a context for the positing of the religious "sense." The requirements of hermeneutics, then, if this "inner process" image is taken as a guide, seem to include a certain predetermination of the character of both text and interpreter, as well as a description of that fundamental phenomenon called "understanding" which is the product of their encounter.

Now, once the notion that "understanding" is the name of a particular phenomenon is brought into question as it is in the work of Wittgenstein, the general quest for the nature of understanding may be replaced by a more limited effort to find and list some of the leading criteria for the employment of the term "understanding" in particular situations. This effort in itself helps to dispel the sense that our various uses of "understanding" comprise a unity rooted in a common proto-phenomenon. But this grammatical unravelling, which separates the criteria of "understanding" from the language of "inner states," so far deals with only one of the two chief aspects of the hermeneutical problem: that is, with understanding as a state or a goal. It offers an answer to the question, "What counts as 'understanding' in this sort of case?" The aspect of the problem which Wach summarizes under the heading of the conditions of understanding remains untouched: "How can one come to understand?" Through what process or activity is one enabled to fulfill the criteria for "understanding," to acquire the ability which these criteria demand? We may still have the suspicion that there is some hidden process, something going on within a person, which enables him to meet the criteria, and that this should be the object of the hermeneutical inquiry. This is the basic phenomenon which is entitled, if anything is, to the name of "understanding."

Grammatical investigation of the "state" of understanding provides an alternative to the effort to describe by one method or another the nature of a phenomenon called "understanding."

It indicates that disputes about the validity of claims to understand may be more profitably settled by referring to acknowledged criteria for the employment of language, rather than by attempting to monitor and to describe something going on within the interpreter. But hermeneutics is not concerned only with the validation of claims to understand, but also with the facilitation of understanding through a disciplined awareness of the conditions of its realization. Can this discussion of the conditions of understanding be carried forward in a way which is consistent with the grammatical investigation of "understanding"--that is, without ignoring its results and reverting to the image of the inner process or proto-phenomenon--and in a way which is practically useful to someone seeking to understand a text?

A central feature of Wittgenstein's grammatical investigation was the change of focus from inner processes to outward circumstances as the criteria for proper employment of terms such as "understanding." Widening the field of investigation, we might ask: Under what circumstances does a person acquire the mastery of a religious utterance (for example) which justifies his saying that he understands it? We may turn from an epistemological concern with transcendental conditions to a concern with empirical, outward conditions: Under what conditions, through what events and activities may one come to understand something? Such an extension of the grammatical investigation might, of course, be seen as only another means of postponing the inevitable confrontation with the epistemological (or phenomenological, or ontological) question of what understanding essentially is. It might, on the other hand, yield results which satisfy the practical intentions of the traditional hermeneutical concern with the conditions of understanding, while permanently avoiding the theoretical problems associated with the traditional, epistemologically-oriented treatment of that theme.

What is needed, then, is a treatment of the conditions of understanding which does not return us to a preoccupation with either the inner nature and situation of the reader, or the inner nature--the "essence"--of the text, but which is rather consonant with the criteria for the employment of "understanding." That is, it should be concerned with the actual requirements, preliminary and procedural, for a person's coming to understand a given range of material. Such a treatment would appear to be more nearly harmonious with the ultimately practical orientation of hermeneutics than those approaches which focus, in one way or another, on the transcendental conditions of the possibility of understanding. But how the former treatment differs from these, and to what extent it is successful, can best be judged after seeing how it might be developed. For this, it is necessary to extend the grammatical investigation--again, building upon Wittgenstein's observations--in close conjunction with Wach's treatment of some of the central features of the hermeneutical concern with the conditions of understanding.

Coming to Understand

One main purpose of Wach's discussion of the conditions of understanding is to state clearly what is *not* required: for example, personal assent to or participation in the religion shaped by the text being interpreted, or the development of an overarching speculative framework into which all religious phenomena may be incorporated. Understanding is equivalent to neither faith nor explanation, for Wach, and to prevent its conflation with either, it is necessary to determine with some care just what its proper conditions and prerequisites are. Hermeneutics has a protective and purifying function. It closes off tempting but illusory shortcuts to understanding, and strives to keep the actual goal in sight and the often difficult path to it clearly marked. This uncompromising, somewhat negative statement of the conditions of understanding is necessarily preliminary to the constructive task of guiding an interpreter to understanding. By establishing some boundaries, it offers a challenge which must be taken up by the second, more positive aspect of the discussion of the conditions of understanding: How is an understanding which preserves the critical freedom of the interpreter and the integrity of the object attainable? Wach perceived this question as one demanding a theoretical solution, and his response was contained in a theory of understanding which showed how the distance between subject and object might be overcome without compromising either. But the question may be differently perceived.

If a person is asked "How did you come to understand X?" he might respond in any of a variety of ways. He might say, for example, "I already understood Y, and X is a variant of that, so it didn't take me long to catch on." Or, "I studied for ten years with the masters, until they were convinced of my proficiency." Or, "I meditated and suddenly it came to me." Each of these accounts might be appropriate in certain circumstances, absurd in others.

Of course, he might instead offer a hypothesis, vague or refined, couched in psychological or philosophical (or even physiological) language, concerning the operation of the faculty of understanding. The inquirer might not know what to do with such a response. He might try to rephrase his question in order to distinguish it from a question about the theoretical foundations of understanding, and to make it clear that he is interested in something else. Ordinarily, a restatement should not be necessary, so the attempt at it is likely to be clumsy and groping: "How did you actually go about getting to understand it? How did you approach it? What did you *do*?" The inquirer is not asking for a theory; he is after some sort of narrative, some account of what is involved in a person's coming to understand in a particular instance. Yet it would not be wrong to say that he is asking about the conditions of understanding.

Some consideration of the conditions of understanding along these lines would not necessarily run into conflict with what Wittgenstein has shown us concerning the use of the concept. It is true that a major result of his grammatical investigation is a clear separation between the criteria for "understanding" and any description--particularly any relying upon the imagery of "inner process"--of what is involved in coming to understand. The maintenance of this distinction suggests the possibility of extricating hermeneutics from the study of human consciousness. But that possibility will not be realized unless it is also possible to discuss the conditions of understanding in a hermeneutically adequate way without falling back upon some sort of philosophical psychology.

Nothing compels us to seek a solution to this problem in Wittgenstein's writings, nor insures that whatever may be found there is significant or adequate in addressing the problem.

But in fact, certain remarks of his on "coming to understand"
are helpful, because they illustrate the sort of non-theoretical
discussion of the conditions of understanding which may provide
a solution.

Wittgenstein says that his own concept of understanding
comprises two kinds of use of "understanding" (or "to understand"), each related to a different way of coming to understand something. There is, first, the sort of case in which a
strange sentence (for example) may be replaced by another which
"says the same." The unfamiliar sentence is transposed or translated into more familiar language and thus rendered comprehensible. Secondly, there is the sort of case in which the unfamiliar sentence cannot be faithfully replace or translated.
Here the reader must be somehow enabled to understand it: he
must be introduced to it, and shown, or taught, or trained, until he masters it on its own terms.[39] Wittgenstein summarizes
both sorts of cases in one remark: "Understanding is effected
by explanation; but also by training."[40] The circumstances of
each deserve some attention.

'"Explanation" can lead to understanding only when the inquirer already possesses a framework into which the strange expression may be placed when translated, or some point of reference with which it may be compared, or some other terms in which
he already understands that which appears to him now in an unfamiliar form. Explanation presupposes a certain capacity, a
preparation or prior familiarity on the part of the interpreter,
then. It also presupposes, of course, that the material to be
understood in this way is not unique; it can be legitimately
compared with, assimilated to, or subsumed under something already understood.

Wittgenstein is not advocating here the sort of explanation of the grammar of a language which he elsewhere rejects
as impossible.[41] Someone asking to have a word explained to
him is not likely to be seeking an ultimate justification or
an etymology accounting for its use. He wants its use clari-
fied in some terms already known to him; a synonymous term of
a fragmentary definition may serve very well. More than that
might be overwhelming, even if it were possible. The sort of
"explanation" to which Wach raises strong objections is also
ruled out by Wittgenstein: explanation cannot produce under-

standing where it presupposes a capacity or a point of contact
which does not exist, or where it does violence to its object
through misrepresentation, reduction, or other distortion.   In
some notes he made upon reading James Frazer's *The Golden Bough*,
for instance, Wittgenstein objected to Frazer's "explanation"
of various aspects of primitive thought and behavior.   Frazer
represents these aspects as based upon erroneous opinions.
He imputes motives to the primitive people based upon his own
cultural background, rather than viewing and describing their
beliefs and conduct in their own context.   To Wittgenstein,
Frazer seems incapable of grasping the possibility of a spiritual life different from that of Englishmen of his own time.
To "explain" the unfamiliar by forcing it into a conceptual
framework which will not accommodate it is not to understand.[42]

For explanation to yield understanding, one must already
possess adequate concepts of capacities into which the object
will fit without distorting strain.   The common difficulties
encountered in translating from one modern language into another
show how rare any such conceptual equivalence is, even in the
least specialized or esoteric areas of human life and communi-
cation.   The translation of religious terms involves particular
problems, as the history of efforts to translate or explain
"Nirvana" or "Tao" to western Christians, or the Christian
"God" to non-Christian Chinese, illustrates.   Concepts characteristic of one cultural or religious tradition often seem to
have no equivalents elsewhere.

If to understand an utterance--from a single word to an
extended discourse--is to know how it is employed, how it affects the fabric of life, what consequences it is to have, then
it may require a particular development of one's conceptual
abilties.   If such growth were impossible, we would be forced
to tailor any unfamiliar utterance to our existing capacities,
by the sort of operation of which Wittgenstein accuses Frazer.
Our understanding of and participation in human life and language presupposes many specific abilities.   "A child has much
to learn before it can pretend," Wittgenstein observes.[43]
Where this sort of prior ability is lacking, the language just
goes past us; we have no place for it, no use for it.   Under
these circumstances, no explanation can succeed in conveying
to us that which we lack.[44]   We need something more.   "One

already has to know (or to be able to do) something in order to be capable of asking a thing's name. But what does one have to know?" Wittgenstein asks. And he concludes: "We may say: only someone who already knows how to do something with it can significantly ask a name."[45]

If we hear echoes of the hermeneutical circle in such remarks, and are tempted therefore to call what is needed a "prior understanding," we must keep in mind that a purely cognitive prerequisite is not intended. It is not a question of the interpreter's needing to have the same type-idea in his mind as that which the utterance represents, or of there being any sort of inner likeness of the utterance in the interpreter's mind. In keeping with Wittgenstein's association of the grammar of "understanding" with that of "ability," it might be helpful--if we succumb to the temptation at all--to think of "prior understanding" in the same way: as a "knowing how," rather than as a body of "knowledge" (types, innate ideas). Wittgenstein suggests thinking of concepts as instruments.[46] We understand them when we know how they are employed. It is not necessary that we have an image or idea in our minds which corresponds to that which is to be understood. The concept may not even allow of representation in any given mode, and if·it does, there may be no correlation between our ability so to represent it and our understanding of it.[47] In any case, what is at stake is the ability.

It is when we do not know what to do with a concept presented to us that explanation may fail, and we must acquire an ability in order to understand. This acquisition of an ability is the form of "coming to understand" which Wittgenstein calls "training."

The word he uses here, *Abrichtung*, is generally used for the sort of training one gives an animal--drilling, conditioning, "breaking in"--rather than for the training one gives a child or adult in various skills; but Wittgenstein's application of the word to human beings in this connection is deliberate.[48] He wants to emphasize the distinction between this procedure and any sort of reasoned explanation. The arbitrary character of linguistic conventions prevents any explanation of linguistic features, except in the sense previously discussed. They can only be shown or described. (Examples are

not an indirect means of instruction for Wittgenstein, as was
seen earlier. Often the example is all we have.) Here, understanding must proceed by demonstration, drill, trial and cor-
rection until the ability to function with the concept is acquired. One is thus given a new capacity through training,
where a more rational appeal might utterly fail. Wittgenstein
gives an example: "How do I explain the meaning of 'regular,'
'uniform,' 'same' to anyone? --I shall explain these words to
someone who, say, speaks only French by means of the corresponding French words. But if a person has not yet got the *concepts,*
I shall teach him how to use the words by means of *examples*
and by *practice*. --And when I do this I do not communicate
less to him than I know myself."[49] Here the contrast between
"explanation" and "training" is clear. It is not that the
teacher has an idea in mind which he is trying to convey to
the learner (or to link to the idea already in the learner's
mind) by means of examples. He is trying to enable the learner
to do something, that is, to achieve a new linguistic capacity.
And that can be done only by showing him how it is done and en-
couraging him to practice until he has it.

Wittgenstein observes that no "logical circle" is presup-
posed in such training. The learner is acquiring something
genuinely new to him.[50] It appears neither necessary nor helpful to invoke any sort of epistemological categories, any account of transcendental conditions, in support of this way of
coming to understand. The imposition of such terms might prove
only confining or diverting, especially if any attempt were
made to structure the activity of understanding in accord with
them. To anticipate a certain kind of result, on the basis of
a theory of understanding, distracts us from the actual task
and may prevent any understanding at all.

Wittgenstein's distrust of speculation or imagination generally as a guide to understanding is emphatic. In one note he
warns, "Philosophers who think that one can as it were use
thought to make an extension of experience, should think about
the fact that one can transmit talk, but not measles, by tele-
phone."[51] Imagination is not a source of information; and in
the unpredictable realm of human linguistic behavior, we need
concrete guidance. Because language is not a strict calculus
whose rules might be implanted in the mind once and for all,

but rather a very loosely related jumble of conventions, we cannot infer and predict with any degree of success, but must watch and follow. "One cannot guess how a word functions. One has to *look at* its use and learn from that."[52] Imagination may only get in the way, as when it imposes a false picture of the grammar of an expression upon us. It may be completely impossible for us to anticipate the employment of an expression, and it is here that sheer "training" or following comes into play.

There is no indication that Wittgenstein's notions of "explanation" and "training" provide an exhaustive account of how one may come to understand something, nor that "explanation" and "training" are mutually exclusive in the attempt to understand a given utterance. Particularly in dealing with a relatively complex object (a religious text, for example), understanding is likely to involve elements of both explanation and training--both assimilation to previously mastered concepts and the extension of one's capacities to master new ones. Wittgenstein's remarks upon these two paths to understanding are instructive, however, because they suggest a way of discussing the conditions of understanding which avoids any indebtedness to an epistemology or a theory of human consciousness, and is consistent with the separation of the criteria for "understanding" from the description of consciousness.

One objection must be confronted. Wittgenstein's appeal to *Abrichtung* is reminiscent of Pascal's appeal to a form of "conditioning" as the only path to faith after rational argument and explanation have been exhausted, in the "wager" portrayed in the *Pensées*. One must submit to drill, and simply behave like a believer, until his passions have been subdued and he becomes docile--conditioned like a domestic beast, accustomed to faith by the force of habit. This passage, and especially Pascal's use of the term "*abêtir*," has always evoked protest. Is reason to be renounced in favor of a blind submission? The exclusion of critical reflection and judgment precisely at the point where greater understanding is sought has important and unpleasant consequences: the abdication of responsibility, vulnerability to any sort of authoritarian direction, the loss of those characteristics which, it is said, distinguish human from animal existence. Wittgenstein's "training," with its similar origins, leaves somewhat the same impression.

Pascal's remarks must be interpreted in the context of his argument as a whole, if one is to see how they are to be taken.[54] A similar weighing of Wittgenstein's references to "training" may be necessary.

It might appear that Wittgenstein has simply concurred with Wach in recognizing the limits of explanation as a means to understanding, but then (perhaps because of his refusal to consider the question of transcendental conditions) has been forced to rely on the other sort of pre-condition Wach wanted to avoid: uncritical acceptance of and participation in that which is to be understood. If we do not already have the capacity to understand something, we can only submit to training until we have it. Wittgenstein's remarks might be construed as lending support to a kind of fideism: One must *become* a Christian (or a Buddhist) if one is to understand the scriptures, creeds, doctrines and so forth which regulate the lives of Christians (or Buddhists). This apparent fideistic tendency has been both criticized and affirmed by Wittgenstein's interpreters, who can appeal to other aspects of his writings besides the treatment of "training" for evidence.

For instance, there is Wittgenstein's remark, "Ordinary language is all right," and his assertion, "Philosophy may in no way interfere with the actual use of language; it can in the end only describe it."[55] Critics who take these to mean that language and its concepts are not to be tampered with, and that we must simply submit to the *status quo* without question, usually go ahead to point out that this is obviously wrong: we *do* criticize our concepts and change our ways of thinking and speaking. Wittgenstein may then be painted as an advocate (or a victim) of a rigid conservatism, bound to a "consciousness" he could not transcend, and ignorant of the possibility and fact of human development through critical appropriation of the past.[56]

In the remarks just quoted, however, Wittgenstein was discussing the function of philosophy as he conceived it; he was not denying that grammar could be criticized or changed, only that it was the role of philosophy to change it, or, especially, to produce an ideal language to take its place.[57] He was not demanding absolute obedience to the tyranny of custom. He was pointing to the conditions of understanding in philosophy: grammar is not understood by stretching it upon a contrived structure of rules, but by paying close attention to individual cases and coming to master them by practice.

In discussing religious belief, Wittgenstein stressed the great difficulty of understanding another person's beliefs, and confessed his own inability to understand some religious concepts.[58] These observations might lend support to a fideistic interpretation of his position also. But they are not conclusive, certainly. "Training" in a religious language may be received through actual participation as a believer in the community whose life is governed by the texts and doctrines to be understood. And perhaps it is realistic to expect the greatest comprehensiveness and depth of understanding to be achieved under such conditions. One writer who draws upon Wittgenstein's work goes on to assert that full understanding, or "mastery," of Christian concepts requires that one submit one's life to regulation by these concepts and in fact "become a faithful individual." One's life must be formed by these concepts; their understanding requires such a degree of self-involvement that it is impossible to withhold personal assent and commitment to them and still understand.[59]

If "training" must take the form of faithful participation, as this suggests, then the sort of objective, critical understanding envisioned by the tradition Wach represents is an impossibility, and those, like Betti, who hope for a revival of that goal face a threat from two directions. Gadamer's challenge to any metaphysical basis for objectivity can be complemented by a Wittgensteinian denial of its practical possibility. However, the equation of understanding with participation which that interpretation of Wittgenstein would require erases an important distinction in Wittgenstein's grammatical treatment of "understanding," which should be examined before it is obliterated.

At one time, when Wittgenstein was initiating his criticism of the "inner process" image of understanding in conversations with the Vienna Circle, he seems to have made the equation just mentioned: understanding is not a process accompanying our linguistic operations; it is those operations

themselves. Understanding *is* the employment of language. In
this way Wittgenstein repudiated the image of understanding as
a separate state or activity beside the actual use of language.[60]
Some time later, however, his alternative was modified, and a
distinction of another sort emerged: He wrote, "'To understand
a word' can mean: to *know* how it is used; to *be able* to apply
it."[61] Understanding is not to be identified with use. It is,
rather, an ability or capacity, which may be exercised or not.
To indicate its grammatical position, we can retain the designation of it as a "state" (*Zustand*) in a hypothetical sense,
realizing that this designation is a grammatical device only.[62]
Understanding is still neither psychic process or behavior; it
is the "state" e.g. of being able to use an expression, or of
knowing how it is used. It need not always issue in a particular sort of behavior, and it is not coextensive with the behavior it enables. There is room, therefore, between understanding
and whatever one goes on to do with it, for critical reflection,
judgment, evaluation, decision.[63] Wittgenstein's later exploration of the grammatical similarities between "understanding"
and other ability-words, discussed in the previous chapter, is
consistent with this distinction.[64]

Wittgenstein's remarks on the subject of understanding suggest that its proper treatment begins with, and largely consists
in, making careful distinctions: distinctions, for example,
among various uses of "understanding"; between some of these
uses and the activity of coming to understand; among various
ways of coming to understand; and between understanding and
either "inner states" or external behavior.

The conflation of understanding with faith or assent--how-
ever closely they may be associated in some areas of ordinary
experience--would contravene several of these distinctions.
It may well be that the majority of persons who come to understand the elements of a religious tradition do so through their
lifelong participation in it, and that other traditions and
doctrines remain closed to their understanding. But this general, *de facto* association of assent and understanding does
not preclude the possibility of someone's achiving a disciplined, critical understanding of the literature and doctrines
of a religious tradition without making that tradition his own.
And here Wittgenstein's discriminating treatment of "under-

standing" is highly useful.

Whatever is eventually decided or discovered concerning Wittgenstein's own views on the problem of understanding religion, his observations on "explanation" and "training" have been helpful in pointing toward the possibility of a discussion of the conditions of understanding which does not require particular epistemological or ontological commitments. This possibility deserves some attention within the context of the hermeneutical discussion.

NOTES TO CHAPTER IV

1. "Verstehen ist selber Geschehen," says Gadamer ("On the Scope and Function of Hermeneutical Reflection," pp. 85-86).

2. Gadamer, *Wahrheit und Methode*, p. xvii.

3. Bultmann, "The Problem of Hermeneutics," p. 252.

4. PI, 255, 133.

5. Stanley Cavell, "The Availability of Wittgenstein's Later Philosophy," *Wittgenstein: The Philosophical Investigations*, ed. Pitcher, pp. 182-185.

6. David Gruender, "Wittgenstein on Explanation and Description," *Journal of Philosophy*, LIX (1962), p. 528.

7. *Ibid.*, pp. 529-530.

8. Hems, "Husserl and-or Wittgenstein," pp. 575-576.

9. Wittgenstein, *Zettel*, 314.

10. "One might say: the axis of reference of our examination must be rotated, but about the fixed point of our real need," says Wittgenstein (PI, 108).

11. Wittgenstein, *Notebooks, 1914-1916*, p. 60.

12. E. D. Hirsch, *Validity in Interpretation* (New Haven: Yale University Press, 1967), p. 4.

13. *Ibid.*, p. 16.

14. *Ibid.*, p. 43.

15. *Ibid.*, pp. x, 43.

16. *Ibid.*, pp. 61, 117.

17. *Ibid.*, p. 207; see also p. 66.

18. The divinatory and comparative functions in Schleiermacher's hermeneutics correspond to the hypothetical and critical functions, according to Hirsch, though Schleiermacher failed to see their proper relationship. Hirsch, *Validity in Interpretation*, pp. 204-206.

19. Hirsch acknowledges the influence of Karl Popper (*ibid.*, xi); certainly the hypothetical-critical model bears some resemblance to Popper's views on the growth of knowledge. See e.g. Karl R. Popper, *Conjectures and Refutations: the Growth of Scientific Knowledge* (N.Y.: Basic Books, 1962), chs. 1 and 10.

20. Hirsch, *Validity in Interpretation*, pp. 142, 206-207.

21. Hirsch, *Validity in Interpretation*, pp. 90-91.

22. *Ibid.*, pp. 49, 51.

23. *Ibid.*, p. 273.

24. *Ibid.*, pp. 76-77, 82-84. "Genre" is Hirsch's preferred term for the general type which must be shared. Pre-understanding is an awareness of the "intrinsic genre" of an utterance (p. 86).

25. *Ibid.*, p. 92.

26. *Ibid.*, pp. 271-272.

27. At the level of verbal meaning, says Hirsch, all types are learned; they are systems of conventions. But since all learning depends upon previous types, typification must be present at the most elementary levels of experience. Hirsch does not say whether he means to suggest some sort of innate type-capacity, and he wants to avoid formal epistemological assertions; but his discussion seems to lead in that direction. The conventionalism he finds in Wittgenstein is inadequate, and must be supplemented by the concept of type. See Hirsch, *Validity in Interpretation*, pp. 66-67, 70-71, 93, 265, 269, 273.

28. *Ibid.*, p. 265.

29. *Ibid.*, pp. 26-27, 242.

30. *Ibid.*, p. 26.

31. *Ibid.*, pp. 265-266.

32. *Ibid.*, p. 26.

33. Wach, *Das Verstehen*, I, pp. 8-9, II, pp. 253-254.

34. Schleiermacher, *Hermeneutik*, p. 55.

35. *Ibid.*, p. 156.

36. Think of the variety of avenues of response opened up by the basic hermeneutical question as it is phrased by a recent writer: "Welche Voraussetzungen müssen gegeben sein, damit ich einen Text verstehe?" (Franz Mussner, "Aufgaben und Ziele der biblischen Hermeneutik," *Was heisst Auslegung der heiligen Schrift?*, [Regensburg: Friedrich Pustet Verlag, 1966], p. 7).

37. The medieval distinction between discursive *ratio* and immediate, intuitive *intellectus*, which in turn has classical roots, is reflected in the dialectic of mediated and immediate components of understanding in modern hermeneutics, according to Emerich Coreth, *Grundfragen der Hermeneutik: Ein philosophischer Beitrag* (Freiburg: Herder, 1969), pp. 55-58.

38. Schleiermacher, *Hermeneutik*, p. 81.

39. PI, 531-533.

40. Wittgenstein, *Zettel*, 186.

41. PI, 109.

42. Wittgenstein, "Bemerkungen über Frazers *The Golden Bough*," pp. 335-338.

43. PI, p. 229.

44. Wittgenstein, *Lectures and Conversations*, p. 53.

45. PI, 30. Similarly: "If you want to understand what it means 'to follow a rule,' you have already to be able to follow a rule" (Wittgenstein, *Remarks on the Foundations of Mathematics*, V, 32, p. 184).

46. PI, 569.

47. "It is no more essential to the understanding of a proposition that one should imagine anything in connexion with it than that one should make a sketch of it," Wittgenstein says (PI, 396).

48. Wittgenstein's use of "*Abrichtung*" is noted by E. K. Specht, *The Foundations of Wittgenstein's Late Philosophy*, p. 66; see also Wittgenstein, *The Blue and Brown Books*, p. 77, and Rush Rhees' remarks in the Preface, p. viii.

49. PI, 208.

50. *Ibid.*

51. Wittgenstein, *Zettel*, 256; see also *Philosophische Bemerkungen*, 66, p. 95, and *Remarks on the Foundations of Mathematics*, I, 98, p. 29.

52. PI, 340.

53. Number 233 in the Brunschvicg edition.

54. See Brunschvicg's note to the passage in Blaise Pascal, *Pénsees et opuscules*, ed. Léon Brunschvicg (Paris: Classiques Hachette, n.d.), p. 441.

55. Wittgenstein, *The Blue and Brown Books*, p. 28; PI, 124.

56. Such criticism and appraisal has been offered e.g. by David Pole, *The Later Philosophy of Wittgenstein* (London: The Athlone Press, 1958), pp. 38-39; Kai Nielsen, "Wittgensteinian Fideism," *Philosophy*, XLII (1967), pp. 193, 208; Karsten Harries, "Wittgenstein and Heidegger: The Relationship of the Philosopher to Language," *Journal of Value Inquiry*, II (1968), pp. 285-286; and (from a Marxist perspective) E. Albrecht, "Zur Kritik der Auffassungen Ludwig Wittgensteins über das Verhältnis von Sprache, Logik, und Erkenntnistheorie," *Deutsche Zeitschrift für Philosophie*, XVI (1968), pp. 828-829.

57. See Stanley Cavell, "The Availability of Wittgenstein's Later Philosophy," pp. 166-167.

58. Wittgenstein, *Lectures and Conversations,* pp. 53, 70.

59. Peter G. Sandstrom, *Language and Conversion: The Logic of Christian Conceptual Training* (Ph.D. dissertation, Yale University, 1970), pp. 166-171, 258. Such a treatment of religious understanding would cohere with Jürgen Habermas' assertion that for Wittgenstein, "understanding language is the virtual repetition of a process of socialization," involving interiorization of norms, repression, and other features of internalized behavior. See Jürgen Habermas, "Zur Logik der Sozialwissenschaften," *Philosophische Rundschau,* Beiheft 5 (1967), pp. 141, 138.

60. Wittgenstein is reported to have said, "Ich verstehe den Satz, indem ich ihn *anwende*. Das Verstehen ist also gar kein besonderer Vorgang, sondern es ist das Operieren mit dem Satz" (Waismann, *Wittgenstein und der Wiener Kreis,* p. 167).

61. Wittgenstein, *Philosophische Grammatik,* I, 10, p. 47.

62. *Ibid.,* I, 41-43, pp. 82-87.

63. The contrast to behaviorism in this respect is noted by Dennis O'Brien, "The Unity of Wittgenstein's Thought," pp. 403-404.

64. It is also in continuity with his statement in *Tractatus Logico-Philosophicus,* 4.024: "To understand a proposition means to know what is the case if it is true. (One can understand it, therefore, without knowing whether it is true.)"

CHAPTER V
CRITICAL UNDERSTANDING IN RELIGION

Theory and Understanding

As a spokesman for the hermeneutical thinkers of the period
from Scheleiermacher to Dilthey, during which hermeneutics took
shape as a reflective discipline, Joachim Wach enunciated three
central principles which should be embodied and brought to realization, he believed, in any mature treatment of hermeneutics.
Each of these has been discussed previously at some length, but
their importance warrants our reviewing them briefly now.

First, hermeneutics has its own determinate range of responsibility. This can be specified in one way by describing
hermeneutics as the connecting link between philosophy and the
individual fields of interpretation; or in another way by saying that hermeneutics has to do with objective understanding--
that is, with the understanding of texts or other specific,
finite material. Hermeneutics is not to lose sight of its proper responsibility, or to forsake the strategic position which
is essential to its functioning. It is a practical discipline,
a servant discipline. The hermeneutician's given task is to reflect upon the problems involved in the interpretation of various sorts of material, and to attempt to resolve some of them
(more precisely: those which seem to arise from confusion or
mistaken ideas about the aims and conditions of understanding)
by offering some positive and defensible account of the nature
of the goal and of the conditions under which it may be attained.
He may draw upon general philosophical resources for clarification and support; he must also give close attention to the
special character of the material with which he is concerned.
But he is not to transform the hermeneutical investigation into
an independent philosophical inquiry, to which textual interpretation is subordinated. Nor may he restrict his attention
to a particular text, or range of material, to such an extent
that his hermeneutical reflection is bound to it and loses any
general validity. Between the general and the specific, the

149

"pure" and the practical, hermeneutics retains a strange independence--so long as it is clear about its fundamental task: to secure and promote objective understanding. This emerges from Wach's study as one major hermeneutical principle.

A second principle is simply a clearer delineation of the meaning of "objective understanding." Objective understanding can be realized only when the independence and integrity of both text and interpreter are recognized and maintained. The text is not to be assigned a meaning. It is to be explicated, understood as its stands, allowed to speak for itself, not manipulated and distorted to fit the reader's purposes.[1] At the same time, objective understanding does not require the reader to surrender his critical intelligence and to take up a fixed position "for" or "against" anything he may find in the text. Of course, the reader cannot simply remain impassive, shutting off his own attitudes and his inevitable responses to the text, and expect it to reveal itself to him. His initiative is vital, and he must involve himself in various ways with the text if he is to discover and trace that form of experience which it expresses and thus to understand it. In fact, only through this sort of sympathetic participation can the reader grant the text its own identity. One who lacks the freedom and flexibility to enter the world constructed in a text, to follow it imaginatively in all its aspects, will probably do poorly as an interpreter.[2] Yet the reader's involvement with the text must be under careful discipline, for the sake of his own critical freedom and for the protection of the independence of the text as well. Both may be too easily compromised.

So from the second principle--the necessity of recognizing and guarding the integrity of both text and reader--a third arises: Hermeneutics must explicate the terms of that interaction between text and reader which permits understanding to be realized. That is, the conditions of understanding must be specified in such a way as to safeguard the objectivity which has been stipulated as essential. From Wach's standpoint, valid, objective understanding must be integral comprehension: it depends upon the integration of a number of elements. The neglect, or the overemphasis, of any of them results not simply in an incompleteness or an imbalance, but often in a more basic misdirection of the interpretation. The whole of human personality must be brought into play in the interpretation of a work, just as it was in its production: the discipline of interpretation, for Wach, involves intellect, affections, and will. All three factors must be taken into consideration in both the empirical and the psychological preparation for integral understanding. The conditions which make objective understanding possible must be searched out and examined; they must be brought into our awareness and related deliberately and productively to one another, if objective understanding is to be defended as a goal and realized in practice.

The three principles may be summarized in a brief statement of the task of hermeneutics: Hermeneutics is concerned with the explication of the conditions which permit the objective understanding of specific human artifacts. Such a statement would seem to embody the characteristic concerns of the hermeneutical development stemming from Schleiermacher--central motifs whose preservation seemed vitally important to Dilthey and to Wach, and whose presence is again being felt in current discussion through the work of Emilio Betti.

Hermeneutics cannot consist simply in the enumeration of canons for the guidance of the interpreter. Such canons may guide the reader through specific practical difficulties encountered in the course of his reading, but if he appeals to them to justify his interpretation as a whole, the canons themselves may easily be challenged; they cannot be used to arbitrate a dispute about the nature and aims of interpretation as a whole, for they are themselves the products of an agreement, a common, received notion, about what interpretation involves.[3] Yet if the canons are laid aside, and a more fundamental, reasoned agreement is sought by means of an epistemological or psychological investigation of the nature of understanding itself, more serious trouble is encountered: First, the conceptual framework within which any such investigation proceeds may require the radical modification or even abandonment of some central notions (such as "objectivity") which the inquiry was meant rather to establish and protect. ("Hermeneutics" itself may be redefined and given an assignment more in harmony with the principles and results of such an investigation.) And secondly, this procedure does not, after all, lead to the desired agreement on generally valid principles. In fact, the more

thorough and detailed the investigation of understanding becomes, the greater also becomes the opportunity for disagree-
ment. Conflicting interpretations may be supported by conflicting accounts of the nature and limits of understanding,
rather than being resolved through the common acceptance of
one unified and unifying account. Wach's refusal to grant a
plenary authority to any particular philosophical school or
system, his insistence on the strange autonomy of hermeneutics,
testifies to his awareness of this danger of the subversion of
hermeneutics by its philosophical helpers. Though the vagueness and generality of his own reconciling approach invites
rather than discourages philosophical explication and criticism, Wach did see the priority of the hermeneutical principles
which he stated, independently of his own contribution, on be-
half of the tradition. The hermeneutical task is a sort of
guardianship: clarifying and stating the objectives of interpretation, and exercising a reflective watchfulness over the
activity of interpretation so that it may lead to an approximation of those objectives.

This note of watchfulness seems fundamentally consistent
with Schleiermacher's aim when he stressed the need for "strict
interpretation" and for a hermeneutical approach which might
support it. Schleiermacher's chief objection to Ernesti, a
leading exponent of grammatical-historical hermeneutics, was
that he took too much for granted, concentrating on the resolution of specific difficulties as they are encountered in
reading, while assuming that understanding will proceed on the
whole "artlessly" and spontaneously. Schleiermacher believed
it essential to reflect upon the entire context and activity
of interpretation, to deal consciously and deliberately with
each element of the situation, and to transform interpretation
into a highly disciplined art.[4] When Wach stressed the interpreter's need to be critically aware of the conditions under
which he is operating, as well as to be clear about his aims,
he is echoing Schleiermacher's concern for a hermeneutical
treatment which would encompass the reader's entire approach to
a text in search of understanding.[5]

How is one to attain this desired clarity concerning the
total enterprise of interpretation--its objectives, its conditions and circumstances? The range of possible approaches

has certainly not been exhausted. Wach chose, however, to use
an approach which seemed to him characteristic, in one form or
another, of the hermeneutical descendents of Schleiermacher.
He chose to attempt to isolate that central, essential element
of interpretation, the proto-phenomenon of understanding; and
then to discuss the task of interpretation in terms of the realization of that phenomenon. The hermeneutician must clarify,
and the interpreter must try to establish, the conditions which
permit understanding to happen. And here already, then, we encounter a subtle but definite separation between the visible
text and its objective treatment, on the one hand, and the operation and object of understanding, on the other; and our attention is focused on the latter. For it is the presence of
that inner phenomenon, and its assiduous cultivation and nur-
turance, which distinguishes the enterprise of interpretation
which the hermeneuticians wish to advance from any number of
other ways of dealing with a text.

Wach spoke out of a tradition which sought to distinguish
the aims and procedures of valid interpretation of human utterances and artifacts from various aims and procedures which might
be appropriate in other areas but which are totally inappropriate to an understanding of the "human world." August Boeckh
and Wilhelm Dilthey were instrumental in developing this distinction in the form in which it came to be used by Wach. For
Dilthey, the human sciences, or *Geisteswissenschaften*, are set
apart from the natural sciences in method, if not always in
material. Many aspects of human life and culture, even of mental and emotional life, are open to examination by the natural
sciences. At the same time, the *Geisteswissenschaften* are not
divorced from the physical realm; rather, they bring to the
study of certain physical phenomena--cultural artifacts, historical events, and other products of the human spirit--a
unique method, that of understanding.

Texts may be manipulated and "explained" arbitrarily as
if they were so much inert material. But they receive proper
treatment only from the reader who is willing to respond to
them on their own terms, according to their own nature. That
responsive treatment is possible only on the basis of the primordial, spontaneous occurrence of understanding, a phenomenon
which is not contrived or arbitrarily invoked, but rather one

which--barring obstacles--naturally characterizes the encounter
between a human being and a product of the human spirit. It is,
as Wach says, a recognition: the intuitive discovery of a pre-
existent inner bond between the reader and that which is embodied in and conveyed by the text.[7] To remove the obstacles
which temporal, cultural, and personal differences put in the
way of understanding, to encourage its presence, and to relate
the bare data of the text to that which is disclosed in understanding, are the tasks of the interpreter. Hermeneutics prepares him by making him aware of those factors which tend to
hinder understanding (e.g. personal and cultural attitudes and
and beliefs, valuations and prejudices) and which must be "paralyzed" or "neutralized" during interpretation, and of those innate positive capacities (e.g. a "sense" for his object, sympathy, imaginative flexibility) which can help him discern the
ultimate meaning embodied in the text, distinguish the essential
from the accidental in its expression, and relate the detail
significantly to the whole.

What is understood on this account, again, is described as
the "meaning" or "essence" or "spirit" of the text. It is only
by a sort of ellipsis that one may speak of "understanding the
text." One understands something in or through the text; this
"something," properly speaking, is the object of understanding.
Text and meaning are not inseparable. In fact, they may be
quite clearly separated. Without understanding, no amount of
labor over a text may tease the meaning out of it. The text
is mute; it might have any of various meanings. The real meaning is connected to it only in the act of understanding. At
the same time, the meaning is not bound to a particular text.
It may find expression elsewhere, perhaps infinitely, though
each different embodiment may produce a somewhat different con-
figuration. In whatever concrete form, the meaning discloses
itself finally only in the event of understanding.

Given this separability of text and meaning, and the absolute centrality of the phenomenon of understanding, it is
perhaps inevitable that there should develop a similar disjunction, or even alienation, between the "outer," empirical work
of textual investigation and the "inner" apprehension of meaning in understanding. This disjunction is clearly evident in
Wach's hermeneutics: despite his affirmation of the need for

harmony between empirical research and the *a priori* dimension, the former receives slight attention within hermeneutics. The proper business of hermeneutics is the explication of objectives and conditions of understanding with regard to a particular kind of textual material. The text and its treatment are not ignored, but rather related to and aligned with what this explication reveals about the way in which meaning is found. When a given image of understanding is developed, it is found to imply a notion of the true object of understanding and also, we might say, of the "true subject" of understanding: of whatever it is about the reader which enables him to understand the object. To these implications about their real identities both text and reader must be reconciled.

Wach sought a foundation for hermeneutical thinking--some firm beginning from which a coherent, comprehensive art of interpretation, comprising the fundamental principles he discerned in the tradition, might develop. He found it in the pervasive image of understanding as a distinctive phenomenon, *sui generis,* universally present as the source of valid interpretation. The unfolding of understanding might be expected to lead to a science of interpretation which would protect and extend the aims of true interpretation, and which would be of such general and obvious validity as to quell the disputes which have marred the history of interpretation.

Is this hope realized? It would appear, on the contrary, that a hermeneutical account thus founded upon an image of understanding may be especially vulnerable both to external criticism and to inner contradictions. The account may be attacked as a whole by those who adhere to rival images of the nature of understanding: the conflict between Wach and Heidegger, or between Betti and Gadamer, begins at this level. To defend an image of understanding against such attack generally involves an appeal to some more fundamental level--say, metaphysics or philosophical anthropology--where agreement is again sought; but this may in turn be rejected. As Wach perceived, the more elaborate the justification offered, the more narrow its appeal. Yet if no response is made to the critic, we are once again faced with a multiplicity of closed hermeneutical systems, and it is up to the interpreter to choose one which is most congenial to his prior aims and his philosophical standpoint.

The ideal of a generally valid, reflective hermeneutics tran-
scending the interpreter's private motives and beliefs has been
lost. Whether or not a philosophical justification for the
hermeneutical position is explicitly invoked in its defense,
the reader soon becomes aware that the hermeneutical account
offered to him has consequences for his view of himself and of
his textual material, at least, if not for his "world-view" or
religious or philosophical outlook as a whole. Hermeneutics
may require him to think, for example, that religious texts are
expressions of religious experience, while his own view of
their nature and origin, individually or in general, may be
quite different. Or hermeneutics may tell him that he shares
a common human spirit, a metaphysical bond, with all mankind;
or that he possesses, however latently, a "religious *a priori*"
or an immediate intuition of ultimate Reality; or require of
him other working assumptions which he may not be willing to
accept. The hermeneutical system, ostensibly a universally
valid and impartial foundation for interpretation, comes to
resemble a doctrine--or, at least, to harmonize well with some
doctrines and to conflict seriously with others.

In addition to the external conflict which ensues as the
hermeneutical account finds its assumptions challenged and must
contend with critics and rivals, some internal difficulties
emerge. If hermeneutics requires of interpreters their prior
assent to some ideas, however, vague or minimal, concerning the
nature of their subject matter, the nature of man, or the nature of language, it not only limits its range of appeal to
those who can give this assent, but it also contradicts its
own fundamental principle that no prior restraints shall be
placed upon the freedom of either text or reader. Of course,
Wach, or any other hermeneutician who bases his work on an investigation and description of the conditions of understanding,
might reply that these are not arbitrary restraints imposed
upon the interpreter in conformity with any external norm.
They are, rather, conditions required by the nature of understanding inself, and binding upon all. In assenting to them,
the interpreter is only acknowledging consciously and dealing
deliberately with the conditions under which understanding
must proceed in any case, and thus gaining some control and
perspective over his interpretation.

But might it not be more accurate to say that these conditions and the interpreter's assent to them are required by the hermeneutician's *image* of "the nature of understanding itself"? The hermeneutician might argue with this revision, if he wants to stress the purely descriptive character of his basic investigation and to avoid any hint of "theorizing" in his work. Nevertheless, he has had to decide at the outset just what it is that he is investigating and describing. He has had to locate whatever it is to which he gives the name "understanding"; and, however amorphous this initial designation of the locus of his work may be, it directs him to certain methods, and not to others, in his search for clarity about understanding, and thus to a certain possible range of results. How closely his hermeneutical account as a whole is bound to the results of his investigation depends partly, of course, on the degree to which the image and its explication actually dominate his thinking, to the exclusion of other concerns. This dominance apparently reaches a culmination in some contemporary hermeneutical thought (especially that of Gadamer), in which the notion of hermeneutics as a methodology or art (*Kunstlehre*) is completely rejected, and with it any hermeneutical norms or principles. Hermeneutics becomes a branch of philosophy.[8]

Wach resisted this development. But in his own work, the tension between the hermeneutical principles he wished to vindicate and the method--the explication of understanding itself --by which he hoped to vindicate them is unmistakable, presaging their separation. The notion of a process of understanding, once accepted and pressed into service as the key to a universally valid, comprehensive hermeneutics, functions like any other key: it unlocks those doors for which it is fitted, and leaves others closed. The hermeneutician, availing himself of the resources thus opened to him, may find his work directed more powerfully by those resources than by any prior criteria he might have had. So, in Wach's work, we find an emphasis on the *a priori* conditions of understanding, a conception of the object of understanding which accords with those conditions, and a relative neglect of questions of objective procedure in dealing with texts. The entire discussion has been shaped by the implications of that image of understanding which was initially accepted and thereby given

considerable responsibility for the structure and content of
hermeneutics.

Understanding as Ability and as Activity

The dissolution of the notion that "understanding" is the
name of a particular thing--an inner process, an experience, a
state of being--obviously has not yet brought the hermeneutical
enterprise to a halt. Hermeneutics has a perplexing ability to
assimilate or to shed potentially destructive ideas: considering the centrality of the notion of understanding to hermeneutics, its apparent imperviousness to criticism of this notion
may seem especially strange. But in fact, there has been a
continual process of criticism and refinement of the concept of
understanding within hermeneutics. Some of the more crude and
troublesome aspects of the prevalent concept have gradually
been eliminated, and hermeneuticians have maintained a high
degree of flexibility in stating and restating their concerns.

Given this flexibility, it is difficult for the critic to
state definitively the problem he would like to expose--the
conceptual error against which he wants to direct his criticism. The notion of understanding is not a Goliath, waiting
to be felled by the analyst's one well-placed shot. It has
taken many forms, has availed itself of various defenses, and
has modified its claims from time to time; there has been no
real unanimity concerning either the ultimate foundations or
the practical yield, the results, of understanding. However
the analyst characterizes the problem, he is likely to find
that his characterization allows the defender of the idea of
understanding to parry his attack by the calm observation that
he has missed the point of the hermeneutical account, and that
hermeneutics has no stake in the misconception he is demolish-
ing.[9]

As each successive hermeneutical thinker, responding to
a new situation, has reconsidered the sources and consequences
of the idea of understanding, perhaps the only constant has
been allegiance to the methodological assumption that the hermeneutical account must be founded upon an investigation of
the nature of the phenomenon of understanding. When faced with
challenges, hermeneuticians have tended to redefine both their

goals and their methods, as necessary, to maintain this relationship between hermeneutics and the study of understanding.
But already in Wach's work--before hermeneutics explicitly assumed the place of epistemology as an inquiry into the transcendental grounds of understanding, as in Gadamer and the post-
Bultmannian theologians--that methodological assumption had
drawn the hermeneutical structure away from those basic goals
which Wach himself had believed most important. We have seen
how such of Wach's aims as objectivity, critical freedom, and
keen respect for the particular were undermined by his account
of the nature and conditions of understanding.

Some later hermeneutical thinkers have been able to deal
with this inconsistency between the practical aims of earlier
hermeneutics and the requirements of the doctrine of understanding by rejecting those aims as impossible or inappropriate, but
in any case bequeathed to modern hermeneutics by a less sophisticated age. Other inheritors of the hermeneutical tradition
(including some engaged in the work of interpretation, as well
as hermeneutical theorists such as Betti) have been unable to
renounce these aims, regardless of the apparent erosion of hermeneutical support for them. Wach observed that hermeneutical
sophistication did not always go together with proficiency at
actual interpretation.[10] We might go farther, and say that
the hermeneutician's separation of the meaning-understanding
phenomenon with which they are concerned from the practical
work of textual criticism and interpretation actually encourages
the alienation of the interpreter from hermeneutics.

The renunciation of the former character and context of
hermeneutics as the *Kunstlehre* of objective understanding, in
favor of an ever more intense concentration upon the phenomenon
of understanding, is a development which may surely be viewed
from more than one perspective. We are told that understanding
is really something quite different from what previous hermeneuticians and interpreters may have thought. In a way, that
observation seems reasonable, almost commonplace: we are increasingly aware of our cultural and historical relativity.
We are awed by the vast distances even between ourselves and
our closest friends. The ideal of objectivity in understanding
seems not only remote, but offensively naive, and the various
metaphysical principles which have been invoked in its defense

do not sustain it against our experience, but are rather implicated in its collapse. We know more about what is involved in
understanding than our predecessors could, and that knowledge
makes it impossible for us to accept their accounts of it.
Perhaps we need to go ahead with the effort to discover what
understanding really is, what it requires and what it can accomplish, even if it means forsaking the practical business of
interpretation.

But what would happen if, instead, we refused to allow this
epistemological development to govern hermeneutics? If the analytic challenge to the notion that "understanding" is the name
of a particular phenomenon has had any impact on us, it should
give us a new perspective from which to view, and to call into
question, the assumption that the hermeneutical uses of "understanding" are to be governed by the results of phenomenological
investigation. Finding and maintaining that perspective may be
difficult, considering the long and intimate association of hermeneutics with epistemology. Any effective critique of that
association must have a constructive aspect: it must at least
point toward the development of an alternative. Otherwise
hermeneutics loses any autonomy, and either is absorbed, by
default, into philosophy, or disappears.

The resources for such a constructive recasting of the
framework of hermeneutics are at hand. Reflection upon the
grammar of "understanding," in Wittgenstein's manner, does more
than simply cast suspicion upon attempts to reify understanding
and discuss its nature; it raises the possibility of other ways
in which "understanding" may be discussed positively. Hermeneuticians might profit from some consideration of these alternate modes.

If we accept as normative Joachim Wach's basic conception
of the role of hermeneutics as the guardian of objective understanding, but cannot accept the image of understanding with
which he operates nor the terms in which that image leads him
to formulate and develop that rule, what possibilities for a
restatement does the foregoing critique provide? Which of
Wach's characteristic emphases can or should be preserved? And
what positive contributions would such a restatement be hoped
to make? Some answers to these questions should emerge if we
approach the inquiry into the nature and conditions of under-

standing with some grammatical observations in mind.

The term "understanding" is often used in connection with various abilities. If a person understands something, we expect that he can do certain things that he might not otherwise be able to do: perform a task, draw a conclusion, conduct himself in a certain way. Often, we expect that he will be able to make make a correct response to an unforseen situation, in which (we might say) he has nothing but his understanding to guide him. He demonstrates his understanding by going ahead correctly on the basis of his own assessment of the circumstances.

We refuse to equate understanding with overt behavior, however. Situations may easily be imagined in which a person behaves as if he understood even though he does not--perhaps by chance, or by imitating someone else. And he who truly understands may nevertheless make a mistake. Further, even a response which demonstrates one's understanding does not necessarily exhaust that understanding. The person who understands may well be aware of a number of options, more or less appropriate to the circumstances, from which he must choose and develop the one which seems most apt. There are a number of points along the way at which this development may take a wrong turn; but even at best, it is unlikely that the result might be said to express or embody his understanding completely.

This relation of understanding to potential has not escaped the notice of hermeneutical writers. Schleiermacher adapted Ernesti's distinction of *subtilitas intelligendi* from *subtilitas explicandi* to separate the process of understanding (which is the concern of hermeneutics) from the concrete results, the expressions, of understanding (which themselves become objects of interpretation).[11] Understanding seems somehow prior to and greater than any particular instance of behavior or utterance which shows understanding. Gadamer makes a similar point when he contrasts understanding with translating. He who understands has a greater freedom than the translator, who is obliged to render an allotted text "word for word" into another form without venturing beyond certain limits, and whose work is then complete. Understanding is never complete, but always underway, leading to new possibilities beyond those which have been set down in any given situation.[12] The attainment of understanding, it seems, gives one a potential which

may never be exhaustively--or perhaps even satisfactorily--
actualized.

It is not difficult for us to imagine then that between
our being addressed by someone or something and our subsequent
behavior--between our meeting with a text, for instance, and
whatever we go on to do with it--something happens "interiorly"
(however the human "interior" is conceived), and it is that to
which we must give the name "understanding."[13] But what if we
refused to locate "the understanding" in this fashion? That
would not necessarily be to deny that there are phenomena associated with our coming to understanding, which may be dis-
dussed under such classic psychological headings as perception,
cognition, and association, or perhaps in some other appropriate language of interiority. It is rather to suggest that to
limit the application of the term "understanding" to whatever
we imagine to be happening there to bridge that gulf between
the mute text and ourselves is an unduly restrictive move,
creating problems which might be avoided.

The transition suggested by the metaphor of "bridging the
gulf" can still be perplexing. Wittgenstein wrote: "Every sign
by itself seems dead. *What* gives it life? --In use it is
alive. Is life breathed into it there? Or is the *use* its
life?"[14] What is it that brings a text to life for us--that
enables us to follow it and to respond to it understandingly?

"Understanding" has something to do with potential, capacity, ability. One way of specifying that relationship is to
say that understanding bestows a certain capacity. A person
is able to do something *because* he understands: first understanding occurs, and because of it one is enabled in new ways.
The presence of understanding is prior to, and responsible for,
the new potential. But the connection of "understanding" with
ability may be portrayed in another way: Understanding does not
bestow an ability; it is an ability. That formulation may be
misleading, however, and is in need of qualification. It is a
remark about the grammar of "understanding," i.e. the functioning of the word in a broad context, and not a statement about
something called "understanding," as "Understanding is a spontaneous event" would appear to be. If it is correct that the
term "understanding" may be used to speak of certain abilities,
then it may be helpful to think of understanding as ability

(or, more cautiously put, of "understanding" as having some functions in common with "ability.")

This alternative has some consequences for hermeneutics. While the first way of connecting "understanding" with ability would encourage us to go behind the abilities, perhaps to go within the interpreter, in search of the basic phenomenon of understanding, the alternative directs us to the interpreter's abilities themselves. The formulation of one aspect of the hermeneutician's task, at least, undergoes a corresponding change: The aims of interpretation can no longer be determined, even ideally, on the basis of a description of the phenomenon of understanding, nor defended by an appeal to such a description. Instead, hermeneutics must attempt to specify the sorts of abilities which might constitute "understanding" in a given situation. That specification can be accomplished by suggesting criteria for "understanding" in various kinds of cases, and it can be defended only in the same way—that is, by appealing to the criteria operative in the situation. Strictly, "defense" is not an appropriate term here: criteria cannot be apodictically imposed and maintained; they must be sought in the interpretative situation.

This approach to the determination of the interpreter's aims may seem to complicate the hermeneutician's work greatly. Perhaps it does. The complication may not be unwarranted, however, nor entirely unanticipated by earlier hermeneuticians. If hermeneutics is to be a "connecting link" between general philosophical reflection and the particular areas of interpretation embraced by various disciplines, this new approach to its task may approximate that position more closely than previous attempts to establish norms for understanding have. Philosophical reflection upon "understanding" produces, not a picture of the nature of understanding which then dominates hermeneutics, but some observations upon the employment of "understanding" and some suggestions concerning the sorts of criteria which may govern its use in different circumstances. But these observations and suggestions are far too broadly scattered and incomplete to constitute anything resembling a general account of "understanding." They have instead a limited, heuristic function: they tell us what kinds of things to consider in seeking to determine the criteria for "understanding"

within particular circumstances. From these circumstances,
then--from a given interpretative situation--we can discern a
more precise range of possibilities. These can be critically
examined and discussed, and a statement of basic criteria governing "understanding" can be initiated.

The interpretation of the Lotus Sutra can again be taken
as an example. What are the aims of interpretation with regard
to this text? If the general norm is derived from a philosophical account of the nature of understanding, then the aim of our
dealing with the text is to produce a certain effect: e.g. for
Wach, recognition. That aim is specified by placing the text
within the category of religious texts: we are to recognize the
religious experience it embodies. The sutra is therefore examined for evidence of the influence of numinous impulses, and
when it is found, the rest of the text is related to it.

The alternative suggested is to derive the norm from the
actual criteria for "understanding." What should a person who
understands this text be able to do? By what criteria might it
be determined that he understands it? Grammatical reflection
suggests that to understand a text is to be able to trace the
implications. But this leaves the field open to a broad range
of possibilities for a more specific statement of criteria.
Both the character of the text and the interests of the interpreter must be considered at this stage, for each may advance,
or exclude, some possibilities.

The question what a text implies is in some respects like
the question what a word or other sign means. Before it can be
answered, it must be determined whose implications would be
considered normative in the situation: whose use of the text
concerns us? If the "authorial will" (to use E. D. Hirsch's
phrase) is designated arbiter, we may run into difficulty with
a text such as the Lotus Sutra, which appears to be a product
of a number of strands or strata of tradition and for which no
individual authors or redactors can now be designated. For
other texts the "authorial will" may be a suitable standard,
but the character of this text excludes that possibility. The
interpreter might, of course, decide to attempt to isolate and
deal with a particular portion or passage of the text in the
hope of recovering its original form and function. But if he
is interested in the text as a unity, in one of it canonical

forms, he must look elsewhere for a standard. He may, for example, aim at understanding the text as it was understood by the earliest communities with which we know it to have been associated, or by later elements of Buddhist tradition, or by some contemporary Buddhists. In each case, the interpreter will achieve understanding to the extent that he discovers what follows from the text for someone--if not the original author, then another designated employer of the text. There may be various ways of understanding the text, then, and no one is inherently preferable to the others. That is not to say that any understanding is as good as any other. Depending on the interpreter's goals, one may be taken as normative while others occupy different places in his perspective and his work. Taking into account the possibilities open to him and his own interests and purposes, the interpreter narrows the range of criteria and stipulates the sort of understanding to be attempted. In this way the hermeneutical standards governing a discipline or an area of interpretation begin to emerge.

These standards are not arbitrary. Their stipulation follows a consideration of relevant aspects of the grammar of "understanding," on the one hand, and an examination of the interpretative situation, on the other, and can be justified in those terms. Conflicts regarding the aims of interpretation cannot be excluded *a priori*, but they can be resolved. The absence of a single standard discourages any ranking (either explicit or subtle) of "levels of understanding" ascending to "true understanding," and gives a new importance instead to the criteria which may actually govern each set of circumstances. To think of understanding in terms of abilities, rather than as an event to be produced or an inner state to be realized, permits hermeneutics to combine a respect for the particular interpretative situation with a concern for commonly accessible criteria for assessing the interpreter's results.

The language of abilities may have a further advantage: It enables us to say without equivocation that the object of understanding--that which is to be understood--is the text. That may appear to be a trivial remark, until we recall the separation between a text and its meaning which a theory of understanding such as Wach's requires. The location of a separable object (e.g. the meaning, essence, type, or spirit) in or behind the text is a consequence of the need to explain the possibility of understanding, when understanding is described as the immediate overcoming of the subject-object gap and the recognition or replication within the interpreter of something vital within the text. This necessary pre-determination of the nature of that which is to be understood in compliance with the terms of a theory of understanding places great restrictions upon the autonomy of the text, subtly erasing the distinction, so important to Wach and his predecessors, between "understanding" and "explanation." But if we use "understanding" in connection with the demonstrable ability to follow a text in its entirety, to unfold its implications in some detail, rather than in connection with the inward realization of an object conveyed by the text, then there is some point to being able to say that what is understood is the text. Whatever its vagaries of structure, whatever its apparent irrelevancies, it is the text itself in its particularity, and not something extracted from it, with which the interpreter must work.

But how is the interpreter's work with the text as such to yield understanding? What enables the interpreter to follow a text at all? If we are not to imagine an "object" within the text which can be intuitively grasped in a moment of understanding, we must find another way to describe how a text may be brought to life. The question is not merely a speculative one; it has a great deal to do with the way in which the interpreter approaches the text--with how he prepares himself, what he does, and what he expects to happen. Yet the status of this question of the conditions of understanding is ambiguous.

The image of understanding as an inner phenomenon (e.g. the recognition of an object) encourages an exploration of the transcendental conditions of the possibility of understanding. How is it that the interpreter is able to perceive the object in this alien collection of signs before him, to extract a meaning from the lifeless text and to realize it within himself? This problem seems to fit within an epistemological framework. Its solution, as Wach saw it, requires the postulation of a latent receptivity within the interpreter to the postulated object within the text. The interpreter's nature, as well as that of the text, must be presumed to fit certain specifications. Hermeneutics thus finds itself dependent upon

a philosophical anthropology. As one consequence, an interpreter may be placed in an intolerable position if hermeneutics
requires his assent to working principles which conflict with
his own beliefs.

For these epistemological assumptions do become working
principles, as Wach's example illustrates, particularly in the
absence of sustained methodological reflection. When the question of the conditions of understanding is treated as an epistemological issue, the results of that treatment tend to dictate
the interpreter's approach to a text in search of understanding,
even where there are other, well-developed methods for objective
textual study. Here the interpreter may experience another division of loyalties: how is he to reconcile the demand for objective, historical-critical study of the text with the more
direct, subjective, intuitive approach which hermeneutics seems
to recommend as the key to understanding? Wach's solution, it
will be recalled, was to regard the objective work upon a text
as preparation for understanding. Autonomous in its own sphere,
it clarifies the historical and cultural circumstances of the
origin of a text, thereby rendering its inner nature more easily
accessible to understanding. Wach was confident that the various critical methods, operating according to their own objective
principles, would lead to that result, correctly setting up the
text for the operation of understanding and incidentally sus-
taining the assumptions concerning the text and interpreter
upon which that operation relies. His faith in the objectivity
and finality of historical-critical study is such that he seems
to think that hermeneutics has no stake in the methodological
problems and discussions within and among the critical disciplines. It accepts the results of critical study, without becoming involved in the fundamental decisions which shape those
results. Focusing its concern upon the *a priori* conditions of
the process of understanding, Wach's hermeneutics ignores the
conditions and assumptions of critical study, and gives us no
basis for a critical assessment of its conclusions as they impinge upon understanding. Hermeneutics thus disclaims any
responsibility for reflecting upon large and decisive aspects
of the interpreter's work.

If we use "understanding" in connection with certain
abilities rather than as the name of a phenomenon, then the

question of the conditions of understanding might be regarded
as a question about the development of these abilities--about
how one may actually come to understand something. This seems
nearer to the interpreter's practical concern, after all: How
am I to go about the task of getting to understand this text?
What preparation do I need, what procedures might I follow?
The interpreter's needs, it would seem, might best be served if
we were to discuss "coming to understand" as an activity, as
purposive behavior, rather than as an inner process. Such an
alternative is preferable not just because it looks practical
and pragmatic and seems to avoid the difficult and distracting
question of the possibility of understanding. Rather, it prom-
ises to resolve two problems created (or at least nourished) by
the traditional hermeneutical approach, and thereby to point
toward a closer realization of the proper role of hermeneutics.

In the first place, a discussion of the activity of understanding can be carried on in a way which does not require sub-
scription to any particular epistemological principles. Statements about what must be the case, in conformity with a doctrine
of understanding, can be avoided in favor of observations upon
the development of those capacities with regard to a text which
can be called "understanding." The hermeneutician, then, need
not ask the interpreter to accept hypotheses (e.g. about the
nature of the material he seeks to understand, about human nature, or about reality in general) which the interpreter may
not be willing or able to accept. Instead, the hermeneutician
helps the interpreter to an awareness of what he needs to do to
achieve an understanding of the material he faces. Hermeneutics
no longer contains any "doctrinal" element which restricts its
validity or usefulness to those who find that element congenial.

The second problem to be addressed by this turn in the
discussion of the conditions of understanding is that of the
long-standing and frequently troublesome dichotomy between the
discursive and the intuitive aspects of interpretation. To
speak of the activity of understanding, and to use that phrase
comprehensively and with consistency, is ultimately to obliter-
ate the distinction between a specification of the conditions
of understanding and a methodology of interpretation. Consequently, "coming to understand" a text can be seen to be in
fundamental unity with the actual work of interpreting it: we

understand a text in and through our dealing with it with a
whole range of techniques of interpretation. It is there that
we learn that mastery of the text which may count as "understanding," if the techniques are employed with that aim in
mind. Tracing the implications of a text is basically an objective, discursive, linear activity. The interpreter's "subjectivity" is by no means unemployed: his experience, imagination, and sensitivity may enable him to discern and to experi-
ment with possible implications, to develop a facility for
discovering and following the threads of a story or an argument,
or to anticipate an author's response to a problem. But there
is no guarantee against his being misled by these personal resources, even so. It is no denial of their importance to refuse to burden them with the weight of a theory of intuition.
They are important just insofar as they contribute somehow to
the activity of interpretation, the more or less deliberate and
methodical business of learning to follow a text. It is in
that total activity--and not simply, or finally, within the
interpreter--that the text is brought to life; for the life of
an utterance is its employment, which we discover by tracing
its implications in particular circumstances.[15] The proper
focus of hermeneutics is upon this activity, then, and the subjective or "psychological" dimension of interpretation may be
taken fully into account as a component of this activity. The
tendency to distinguish the process of understanding from the
interpreter's activity, and to discuss it in separate terms,
should not persist. To discuss the conditions of understanding
is to discuss the total work of interpretation.

Hermeneutics and Interpretation

How is this hermeneutical discussion of interpretation to
be approached? Its terms are not to be dictated by a theory
of understanding, as if hermeneutics were a mediating level between epistemological theory and interpretative practice. Its
role as a "connecting link" is to be affirmed, but differently
construed. The notion that epistemology should serve as a
guide to the practice of interpretation is corollary to the
idea that it is the task of epistemology to define "understanding" and to establish generally valid norms for the use of the

term. If hermeneutics rejects the latter, and seeks instead to determine the criteria for "understanding" from its actual employment (that is, on grammatical rather than epistemological grounds), then the former notion is also called into question. Hermeneutics is not a link between theory and practice. It is, rather, a kind of reflection upon interpretation which attempts to relate the aims of interpretation in a given field to the relevant criteria for "understanding," and then to bring these criteria to bear upon the activity of interpretation so as to provide a focal point for the integration and direction of the procedures of interpretation.

How might that sort of reflection be carried out in regard to the interpretation of religious material?

One of the first facts to note is that hermeneutics then neither requires not offers any definition of "religion" or "religious." For Wach, such a normative prior conception was finally inescapable: all religious material testifies to a common origin in religious experience, and interpretation must begin with the recognition of this inherent character. Interpretation depends upon the fact that a text may be "placed" according to the aspect of the human *a priori* (in this case, religious experience) to which its gives concrete expression. Although Wach rejected the idea that an externally imposed, theoretically-grounded definition of the subject matter could serve as a valid basis for "descriptive-understanding" interpretation, his model of understanding made its own demands of the material. But if hermeneutics is freed from that sort of model, the interpreter, in turn, is free to delimit the range of his inquiry according to other considerations. Hermeneutics as such neither defines his subject matter initially, nor informs his subsequent judgments or theories concerning what he has understood.

To insist on this distance between hermeneutics and theoretical reflection on religion is not merely negative. It may be only when hermeneutics keeps its distance from theory in that way that it can attain an intimate and productive relationship with the work of interpretation, in which theorizing may have a positive role in concert with many other methods. Hermeneutical reflection should enable the interpreter to reach some clarity concerning his aims and interests in interpretation (among many possible aims and interests), and to choose and employ procedures which are consistent with those aims. Commensurate with his responsibility for clarifying his goals is his freedom and flexibility in the use of whatever procedures are available to him for attaining those goals.

In the Epistle to the Galatians, for example, the interpreter encounters this passage: "I have been crucified with Christ; it is no longer I who live, but Christ who lives in me" (Gal. 2:20). How is that to be understood? If the interpreter is interested in investigating the personality of Paul, or his religious experience, or first-century religious experience generally, that utterance might be useful evidence. (So may much of the New Testament be used as resource material for the study of personality or of social institutions: economics, slavery, law.) If the interpreter wants to know what the text has meant to other people, he may study the history of its interpretation and its use in theology and devotion in the particular periods or traditions with which he may be concerned. But if he wants to understand the text as it was employed by Paul--that is, to understand the author's own use of his words --then his efforts will be directed toward the discovery of the implications of the utterance. Rather than trying to go behind the text, he will attempt to follow the text; the text itself is the object of understanding, not a means of understanding something else. So the interpreter will not begin by categorizing the text as, say, a religious utterance, or an expression of Paul's personality or existential condition. No "prior understanding" of the text *as* a certain kind of utterance is required--though, of course, various possibilities may be entertained at some stage of interpretation in the effort to draw out the implications of the passage.

In fact, every tool and technique of interpretation will be directed explicitly toward understanding--that is, toward the interpreter's gaining a mastery of the implications of the text. The activity of interpretation involves a connection of hypothesis and investigation, through which the interpreter may gradually gain and sharpen his ability to follow the text. Leading questions may help to explicate what is implicit: When Paul speaks of being "crucified," is he referring his readers to a particular event or experience in his life? When he says that Christ lives in him, is this to be taken as a mystical

union, or an ontological identity? Is it an exclusive relationship? And what follows from it: is Paul claiming Christ's
authority, or is he negating his own will? This sort of questioning, which ranges from the more crude and naive to the
more sensitive and discriminating, and from vague guesses to
more clear hypotheses, opens up possibilities which must then
be tested. Each question might represent a "prior understanding," a conjecture as to the employment of the utterance, though
it is doubtful whether anything would be gained by the use of
that phrase. The possibility contained in each question may
be confirmed, refined, refuted, or simply left open, by subsequent investigation.

The various investigative procedures, then, come to be
seen as integral elements in the activity of coming to understand the text. Establishing the authenticity and original
form of the Epistle (and the position of this passage within
it), its relationship to other Pauline writings, and the circumstances of its writing; studying the Epistle as a whole,
and assessing the role of this passage in the development of
the author's themes or arguments; looking for parallels and
analogies in Paul's other writings; perhaps examining other
contemporary Christian or non-Christian writings for similar
passages; studying the tradition of interpretation; all of
these activities and more, in concert, help the interpreter to
discern the implications of the text. None of these activities
are mechanical operations. In their selection and initiation,
in their pursuit, and in the weighing and combining of their
results, the interpreter must draw upon his own resources constantly in making decisions. Moreover, it is precisely in and
through this complex and demanding activity that the interpreter develops his understanding of the passage. As he discovers its range of implication, learns that some kinds of
questions are relevant and helpful in elucidating the text
while others are not, and begins to see what differences the
text makes and where its impact is, he is attaining that mastery of the text which may count as "understanding" according
to the criteria he has acknowledged at the outset. The adequacy of his understanding depends considerably upon the extent
to which he has been directed, in his interpretation, by those
criteria, and has reflected upon the relationship of his activity

to his goals. It is this actual work upon the text which builds understanding; and hermeneutical reflection must be engaged at every point of the work.

If hermeneutics is separated from the theory of understanding, as has been suggested here, then the role of theory *in* understanding is considerably modified. When hermeneutics does not insist that the work of interpretation be prefaced and guided by (and perhaps limited and transcended by) particular prior views of the subject matter or "object," or of the nature or existential situation of the interpreter himself, the way is clear for a much more flexible and potentially productive use of theories—and of the interpreter's personal resources as well— in interpretation. The interpreter is free to entertain and explore many different possibilities, submitting each as a question to the text. The text is not used to confirm the theory; the theory, as question, may be used to draw out and explicate the text. Similarly, the interpreter's personal response to the text at any point during his inquiry is not isolated and prized in itself as the product of interpretation, but it can engender new possibilities, new approaches or questions to be integrated once again into the activity of interpretation. In this way the reader's responses to a text may mature along with, and contribute to the maturation of, his understanding of it.

At the same time, the necessary formal separation of understanding and response may be maintained. During interpretation, response is subordinated to the activity of understanding and is pressed into its service whenever possible: the theories, conjectures, associations, and reactions provoked by the text are neither suppressed nor glorified, but rather put to work. Their controlled use in this way should lead to no confusion of response with understanding, if the criteria for "understanding" are kept in mind. (Here Wittgenstein's distinctions, mentioned at the close of the previous chapter, may be helpful.) Nor does this occasional use exhaust the function of the interpreter's response to the text, as if it were only instrumental to understanding. It is on the basis of an achieved understanding of a text that a more finished response may properly take place: here, the interpreter uses his understanding of the text for some further purpose, such as theological reflection, comparison with other writings, or any of various kinds of criticism or appropriation of the text.

Perhaps the basic function of hermeneutics in interpretation, then, is one of restraint. Hermeneutics is neither doctrine not method. It does not provide a shortcut to understanding, nor guarantee results. Hermeneutics comprises, first, the discovery and clarification of criteria for "understanding," and secondly, the direction of the methods and techniques used in the activity of interpretation toward the realization of those criteria. It is not a body of principles to be applied to a text, but a discipline of reflection upon the aims and activities of interpretation. In both its normative and its methodological aspects, hermeneutics is less reassuring than warning: it reminds us of the complexities and difficulties of understanding, and insists that the entire activity of interpretation be consciously referred to its aims.[16]

The program for hermeneutics which has been suggested here as an alternative to that represented by Wach bears the promise of realizing three principal goals. The first is the affirmation of the freedom of the interpreter. He is not required to assent to any prior understanding of his textual material, nor to any prior understanding of himself, which might conflict with his own beliefs (or lack of beliefs) concerning either, or which contains an implicit doctrine potentially leading to such conflict. Understanding does not begin with a "metaphysical decision," and hermeneutics is not predicated upon one. Nor does hermeneutics interfere with the interpreter's freedom to go beyond understanding to judgment and criticism. "Understanding" is clearly separable from "faith."

The second goal is the protection of the integrity and identity of the text. No binding prior understanding of the nature of the text (or of the nature of the object of understanding, conceived as separable from the text) is imposed by hermeneutics as a condition of understanding. The text is the object of understanding, and its character is disclosed in and through the work of interpretation.

The realization of the third goal is a consequence of this recognition of the centrality of the text, as text, in understanding: Hermeneutics may be closely coordinated with the concrete work of interpretation. It provides a focus for an inquiry, a point of orientation and coherence for the methods and activities involved in the exploration of a text. Hermeneutics relates the achievement of understanding directly to the activity of interpretation.

These, of course, were the goals of Joachim Wach, and of the hermeneutical tradition he wished to epitomize. The foregoing critique has concentrated upon some problems in that tradition, as Wach represented it, having to do with the concept of understanding and its treatment in hermeneutics. The reflections of Ludwig Wittgenstein upon that concept were considered in the hope that they might clarify the character of these difficulties. In order to appraise these reflections in their own right, it was necessary to separate this consideration from two recent approaches to Wittgenstein's work: one would subordinate it to phenomenology or to hermeneutical philosophy, while the other would use his work to support the conflation of understanding and assent. Wittgenstein's discriminating treatment of the concept, taken on its own terms, was found to be both critically and constructively helpful; it was possible then to go beyond an analysis of the problems to suggest a different approach to the goals of hermeneutics.

This critique might therefore be considered to be in basic continuity with the aims of the hermeneutical tradition.

NOTES TO CHAPTER V

1. The distinction between *Sinngebung* and *Auslegung* is bor-
    rowed from Betti (*Die Hermeneutik*, pp. 30-31) as a recent
    expression of the concern Wach wished to emphasize.

2. Cf. Schleiermacher, *Hermeneutik*, pp. 72-73.

3. G. F. Seiler, a hermeneutician of the grammatical-histor-
    ical school who explicitly defends hermeneutics as "a
    collection of rules," nevertheless precedes this defini-
    tion with several paragraphs which set forth a general
    theory of language, meaning and understanding--the received
    axioms from which the rules naturally proceed. See George
    Frederic Seiler, *Biblical Hermeneutics: or, the Art of
    Scripture Interpretation*, tr. William Wright (London:
    Frederick Westley and A. H. Davis, 1835), pp. 23-27.
    Seiler's observations are closely related to the similarly
    open and undefended assumptions of Ernesti; see J. A.
    Ernesti, *Elements of Interpretation*, tr. with notes by
    Moses Stuart, 3rd ed. (Andover: Flagg and Gould, 1824),
    esp. pp. 7-9.

4. Schleiermacher, *Hermeneutik*, pp. 28-30; on Schleiermacher's
    reaction to Ernesti, see Dilthey, *Leben Schleiermachers*,
    II, pp. 684-689.

5. Wach, *Das Verstehen*, II, pp. 9-10.

6. See Wilhelm Dilthey, "Abgrenzung der Geisteswissenschaften,"
    Gesammelte Schriften, VII, pp. 79-88.

7. Wach's fundamental dependence upon Boeckh for his concept
    of "recognition" as the kernel of understanding is sug-
    gested in a recent article by Joseph M. Kitagawa, "*Verstehen*
    and *Erlösung*: Some Remarks on Joachim Wach's Work," *His-
    tory of Religions*, XI (1971), p. 37.

8. See Kimmerle, "Hermeneutische Theorie oder ontologische
    Hermeneutik," p. 121; cf. Theodore Kisiel, "The Happening
    of Tradition: The Hermeneutics of Gadamer and Heidegger,"
    Man and World, II (1969), pp. 360-361, on the transforma-
    tion. Gadamer says (in *Wahrheit und Methode*, p. 167)
    that Schleiermacher's retention of the term *Kunstlehre*
    for his approach should not obscure the great difference
    between his work and previous hermeneutics. The trans-
    formation from methodology to philosophy has already begun.

9. Thus Howard Nelson Tuttle, *Wilhelm Dilthey's Philosophy
    of Historical Understanding: A Critical Analysis* (Leiden:
    E. J. Brill, 1969), ch. 5, responds on Dilthey's behalf
    to a generalized positivist attack on the concept of *Ver-
    stehen*. Cf. Jane R. Martin, "Another Look at the Doctrine
    of Verstehen," *British Journal for the Philosophy of
    Science*, XX (1969), pp. 53-67.

10. Wach, *Das Verstehen*, III, pp. 300-301.

11. Schleiermacher, *Hermeneutik,* p. 31.

12. Hans-Georg Gadamer, "Martin Heidegger und die Marburger Theologie," *Zeit und Geschichte: Dankesgabe an Rudolf Bultmann zum 80. Geburtstag,* ed. Erich Dinkler (Tübingen: J. C. B. Mohr [Paul Siebeck], 1964), p. 490. Whether Gadamer does justice here to the translator and his task is doubtful; but that was not his object.

13. If the idea of understanding as a subjective or interior phenomenon is rejected (as by Gadamer, who locates it rather at the "fusion of horizons"), then the language of interiority is strictly inappropriate, and the event must be described in other terms.

14. PI, 432.

15. A single word (e.g. "right") or a natural symbol (e.g. a dove), whatever immediate and apparently obvious associations it may convey to us, "lives" only in particular uses. Our associations may help us discover its use in a given case, or they may as easily block that discovery by blinding us to novelty. A more complex utterance is not necessarily any less ambiguous. The interpreter must know how to put his reactions to work without relying on them or subordinating his reading of circumstances to them.

16. This restraining function is not inconsistent with Schleiermacher's concept of the "*strengere Praxis*" which hermeneutics is to advocate. See *Hermeneutik,* p. 86.

BIBLIOGRAPHY

Abel, Theodore. "The Operation Called *Verstehen*." *Readings in the Philosophy of Science*. Edited by Herbert Feigl and May Brodbeck. N.Y.: Appleton-Century-Crofts, 1953.

Albrecht, E. "Zur Kritik der Auffassungen Ludwig Wittgensteins über das Verhältnis von Sprache, Logik, und Erkenntnistheorie." *Deutsch Zeitschrift für Philosophie*, XVI (1968), pp. 813-829.

Albritton, Rogers. "On Wittgenstein's Use of the Term 'Criterion.'" *Wittgenstein: The Philosophical Investigations*. Edited by George Pitcher. Garden City, N.Y.: Doubleday & Company, Anchor Books, 1966.

Apel, Karl-Otto. *Analytic Philosophy of Language and the Geisteswissenschaften*. Translated by Harold Holstelilie. Foundations of Language, Supplementary Series, IV. Dordrecht: D. Reidel Publishing Company, 1967.

_____. "Das Verstehen (eine Problemgeschichte als Begriffsgeschichte)." *Archiv für Begriffsgeschichte*, I (1955), pp. 142-199.

_____. "Wittgenstein und das Problem der hermeneutischen Verstehens." *Zeitschrift für Theologie und Kirche*, LXIII (1966), pp. 49-87.

Bell, Richard H. *Theology as Grammar: Uses of Linguistic Philosophy for the Study of Theology with Special Reference to Ludwig Wittgenstein*. Ph.D. dissertation, Yale University, 1968.

_____. "Wittgenstein and Descriptive Theology." *Religious Studies*, V (1969), pp. 1-18.

Betti, Emilio. *Die Hermeneutik als allgemeine Methodik der Geisteswissenschaften*. Philosophie und Geschichte, 78/79. Tübingen: J. C. B. Mohr (Paul Siebeck), 1962.

Bolle, Kees W. "Jan de Vries (1890-1964)." *History of Religions*, V (1965), pp. 173-177.

_____. "Wach's Legacy: Reflexions on a New Book." *History of Religions*, X (1970), pp. 80-90.

Braaten, Carl E. *History and Hermeneutics*. New Directions in Theology Today, edited by William Hordern, II. Philadelphia: Westminster Press, 1966.

Bultmann, Rudolf. "Is Exegesis Without Presuppositions Pos-
        sible?" *Existence and Faith: Shorter Writings of
        Rudolf Bultmann*. Selected, translated, and intro-
        duced by Schubert M. Ogden. Cleveland: World Pub-
        lishing Company, 1960.

_____. "The Problem of Hermeneutics." *Essays, Philosophical
        and Theological*. Translated by C. G. Greig. N.Y.:
        Macmillan Company, 1955.

Cain, Seymour. Review of *The Comparative Study of Religions*,
        by Joachim Wach. *Journal of Religion*, XL (1960),
        pp. 47-49.

Cavell, Stanley. "The Availability of Wittgenstein's Later
        Philosophy." *Wittgenstein: The Philosophical In-
        vestigations*. Edited by George Pitcher. Garden
        City, N.Y.: Doubleday & Company, Anchor Books, 1966.

Cook, John W. "Human Beings." *Studies in the Philosophy of
        Wittgenstein*. Edited by Peter Winch. London:
        Routledge & Kegan Paul, 1969.

Coreth, Emerich. *Grundfragen der Hermeneutik: Ein philoso-
        phischer Beitrag*. Freiburg: Herder, 1969.

Cullmann, Oscar. *Salvation in History*. Translated by Sidney
        G. Sowers. N.Y.: Harper & Row, 1967.

Desroche, Henri. "Sociologie et theologie dans la typologie
        religieuse de Joachim Wach." *Archives de sociolo-
        gie des religions*, I (1956), pp. 41-63.

Dilthey, Wilhelm. "Abgrenzung der Geisteswissenschaften."
        Gesammelte Schriften, VII. Edited by B. Groethuysen.
        Leipzig: B. G. Teubner Verlag, 1927.

_____. "Die Entstehung der Hermeneutik." *Gesammelte
        Schriften*, V. Edited by Georg Misch. Leipzig: B.
        G. Teubner Verlag, 1924.

_____. *Leben Schleiermachers*, II. *Gesammelte Schriften*,
        XIV. 2 half-volumes. Edited by Martin Redeker.
        Göttingen: Vandenhoek & Ruprecht, 1966.

_____. "Das Problem der Religion." *Gesammelte Schriften*,
        VI. Edited by Georg Misch. Leipzig: B. G. Teubner
        Verlag, 1924.

_____. "Die Typen der Weltanschauung und ihre Ausbildung
        in den metaphysischen Systemen." *Gesammelte
        Schriften*, VIII. Edited by B. Groethuysen.
        Leipzig: B. G. Teubner Verlag, 1931.

_____. "Das Verstehen anderer Personen und ihrer Leben-
        säusserungen." *Gesammelte Schriften*, VII. Edited
        by B. Groethuysen. Leipzig: B. G. Teubner Verlag,
        1927.

Ebeling, Gerhard. "Word of God and Hermeneutics." *Word and Faith*. Translated by James W. Leitch. Philadelphia: Fortress Press, 1963.

Eliade, Mircea. "History of Religions and a New Humanism." *History of Religions*, I (1961), pp. 1-8.

_____. "On Understanding Primitive Religions." *Glaube, Geist, Geschichte: Festschrift für Ernst Benz zum 60. Geburstag am 17. November 1967*. Edited by Gerhard Müller and Winfried Zeller. Leiden: E. J. Brill, 1967.

Ernesti, J. A. *Elements of Interpretation*. Translated with notes by Moses Stuart. 3rd ed. Andover: Flagg and Gould, 1824.

Fahrenbach, Helmut. "Die logisch-hermeneutische Problemstellung in Wittgensteins 'Tractatus.'" *Hermeneutik und Dialektik*, II. Edited by Rüdiger Bubner *et al*. Tübingen: J. C. B. Mohr (Paul Siebeck), 1970.

Fann, K. T. *Wittgenstein's Concept of Philosophy*. Oxford: Basil Blackwell, 1969.

Fehl, Noah Edward. Review of *Types of Religious Experience: Christian and Non-Christian*, by Joachim Wach. *Anglican Theological Review*, XXXV (1953), pp. 276-278.

Gadamer, Hans-Georg. "Martin Heidegger und die Marburger Theologie." *Zeit und Geschichte: Dankesgabe an Rudolf Bultmann zum 80. Geburtstag*. Edited by Erich Dinkler. Tübingen: J. C. B. Mohr (Paul Siebeck), 1964.

_____. "On the Scope and Function of Hermeneutical Reflection." *Continuum*, VIII (1970), pp. 77-95.

_____. "Die Phänomenologische Bewegung." *Philosophische Rundschau*, XI (1963), pp. 1-45.

_____. "The Problem of Language in Schleiermacher's Hermeneutic." Translated by David E. Linge. *Schleiermacher as Contemporary*. Journal for Theology and Church, edited by Robert W. Funk, VII. N.Y.: Herder and Herder, 1970.

_____. *Wahrheit und Methode*. 2nd ed. Tübingen: J. C. B. Mohr (Paul Siebeck), 1965.

Gallie, W. B. *Philosophy and the Historical Understanding*. 2nd ed. N.Y.: Schocken Books, 1968.

Garver, Newton, "Analyticity and Grammar." *The Monist*, LI (1967), pp. 397-425.

_____. *Grammar and Criteria*. Ph.D. thesis, Cornell University, 1965.

_____. "Wittgenstein on Criteria." *Knowledge and Experience.* Edited by C. D. Rollins. Pittsburgh: University of Pittsburgh Press, 1962.

Goff, Robert A. "The Wittgenstein Game." *The Christian Scholar,* XLV (1962), pp. 179-197.

Gosselin, M. "Enkele Beschouwingen naar Aanleiding van 'Language as Hermeneutic in the Later Wittgenstein.'" *Tijdschrift voor Filosofie,* XXVIII (1966), pp. 72-83.

Gruender, David. "Wittgenstein on Explanation and Description." *Journal of Philosophy,* LIX (1962), pp. 523-530.

Gustafson, Donald. "On Pitcher's Account of *Investigations* 43." *Philosophy and Phenomenological Research,* XXVIII (1967), pp. 252-258.

Habermas, Jürgen. "Zur Logik der Sozialwissenschaften." *Philosophische Rundschau,* Beiheft 5 (1967).

Hallie, Philip. "Wittgenstein's Grammatical-Empirical Distinction." *Journal of Philosophy,* LX (1963), pp. 565-578.

Harries, Karsten. "Wittgenstein and Heidegger: The Relationship of the Philosopher to Language." *Journal of Value Inquiry,* II (1968), pp. 281-291.

Heidegger, Martin. *Being and Time.* Translated by John Macquarrie and Edward Robinson. N.Y.: Harper & Row, 1962.

Hems, John M. "Husserl and-or Wittgenstein." *International Philosophical Quarterly,* VIII (1968), pp. 547-578.

Hirsch, E. D. *Validity in Interpretation.* New Haven: Yale University Press, 1967.

Hodges, H. A. *The Philosophy of Wilhelm Dilthey.* London: Routledge & Kegan Paul, 1952.

_____. *Wilhelm Dilthey: An Introduction.* London: Routledge & Kegan Paul, 1944.

Hunter, J. F. M. "'Forms of Life' in Wittgenstein's *Philosophical Investigations.*" *American Philosophical Quarterly,* V (1968), pp. 233-243.

James, E. O. Review of *The Comparative Study of Religions,* by Joachim Wach. *Church Quarterly Review,* CLX (1959), pp. 533-534.

Käsemann, Ernst. "Zum Thema der urchristlichen Apokalyptik." *Zeitschrift für Theologie und Kirche,* LIX (1962), pp. 257-284.

Kerr, F. "Language as Hermeneutic in the Later Wittgenstein."

Tijdschrift voor Filosofie, XXVII (1965), pp. 491-520.

_____. "Reply to M. Gosselin." *Tijdschrift voor Filosofie,* XXVIII (1966), pp. 84-89.

Kimmerle, Heinz. "Hermeneutische Theorie oder ontologische Hermeneutik." *Zeitschrift für Theologie und Kirche,* LIX (1962), pp. 114-130.

Kisiel, Theodore. "The Happening of Tradition: The Hermeneutics of Gadamer and Heidegger." *Man and World,* II (1969), pp. 358-385.

Kitagawa, Joseph M. "Joachim Wach and Sociology of Religion." *Journal of Religion,* XXXVII (1957), pp. 174-188.

_____. "Primitive, Classical, and Modern Religions: A Perspective on Understanding the History of Religions." *The History of Religions: Essays on the Problem of Understanding.* Edited by Joseph M. Kitagawa. Essays in Divinity, I. Chicago: University of Chicago Press, 1967.

_____. "*Verstehen* and *Erlösung:* Some Remarks on Joachim Wach's Work." *History of Religions,* XI (1971), pp. 31-53.

Long, Charles H. "Prolegomenon to a Religious Hermeneutic." *History of Religions,* VI (1967), pp. 254-264.

Malcolm, Norman. *Ludwig Wittgenstein: A Memoir.* With a Biographical Sketch by Georg Henrik von Wright. N.Y.: Oxford University Press, 1962.

Martin, Jane R. "Another Look at the Doctrine of Verstehen." *British Journal for the Philosophy of Science,* XX (1969), pp. 53-67.

Moore, G. E. "Wittgenstein's Lectures in 1930-33." *Philosophical Papers.* N.Y.: Collier Books, 1962.

Mussner, Franz. "Aufgaben und Ziele der biblischen Hermeneutik." Wilfried Joest, *et al. Was heisst Auslegung der heiligen Schrift?* Regensburg: Friedrich Pustet Verlag, 1966.

Niebuhr, H. Richard. "Review of *Sociology of Religion,* by Joachim Wach. *Theology Today,* II (1945), pp. 409-411.

Nielsen, Kai. "Wittgensteinian Fideism." *Philosophy,* XLII (1967), pp. 191-209.

O'Brien, Dennis. "The Unity of Wittgenstein's Thought." *Ludwig Wittgenstein: The Man and His Philosophy.* Edited by K. T. Fann. N.Y.: Dell Publishing Company, 1967.

O'Dea, Thomas F. *Sociology and the Study of Religion: Theory, Research, Interpretation.* N.Y.: Basic Books, 1970.

Oxtoby, Willard Gurdon. "*Religionswissenschaft* Revisited." *Religions in Antiquity: Studies in Memory of Erwin Ramsdell Goodenough.* Edited by Jacob Neusner. Studies in the History of Religions, Supplements to *Numen*, XIV. Leiden: E. J. Brill, 1968.

Palmer, Richard E. *Hermeneutics.* Evanston: Northwestern University Press, 1969.

_____. "Hermeneutics and Methodology." *Continuum*, VII (1969), pp. 153-158.

Pascal, Blaise. *Pensées et opuscules.* Edited by Léon Brunschvicg. Paris: Classiques Hachette, n.d.

Pitcher, George. *The Philosophy of Wittgenstein.* Englewood Cliffs, N.J.: Prentice-Hall, 1964.

Pole, David. *The Later Philosophy of Wittgenstein.* London: The Athlone Press, 1958.

Popper, Karl R. *Conjectures and Refutations: The Growth of Scientific Knowledge.* N.Y.: Basic Books, 1962.

Rankin, K. W. "Wittgenstein on Meaning, Understanding, and Intending." *American Philosophical Quarterly*, III (1966), pp. 1-13.

Rhees, Rush. "Can There Be a Private Language?" *Discussions of Wittgenstein.* London: Routledge & Kegan Paul, 1970.

Robinson, James M. "Hermeneutic Since Barth." *The New Hermeneutic.* New Frontiers in Theology, II. Edited by James M. Robinson and John B. Cobb, Jr. N.Y.: Harper & Row, 1964.

Robinson, Richard H. Review of *The Comparative Study of Religions,* by Joachim Wach. *Canadian Journal of Theology*, VIII (1962), pp. 57-59.

Rudolph, Kurt. "Leipzig und die Religionswissenschaft." *Numen*, IX (1962), pp. 53-68.

_____. *Religionsgeschichte an der Leipziger Universität und die Entwicklung der Religionswissenschaft.* Sitzungsberichte der Sächsischen Akademie der Wissenschaften zu Leipzig, Philologisch-historische Klasse, 107:1. Berlin: Akademie-Verlag, 1962.

_____. Review of *Vergleichende Religionsforschung* (translation of *The Comparative Study of Religions*), by Joachim Wach. *Theologische Literaturzeitung*, LXXXIX (1964), pp. 346-349.

Sandstrom, Peter Gerhard. *Language and Conversion: The Logic of Christian Conceptual Training.* Ph.D. dissertation, Yale University, 1970.

Scheimann, Richard William. *Wach's Theory of the Science of Religion.* Ph.D. dissertation, University of Chicago, 1963.

Schleiermacher, Fr. D. E. *Hermeneutik.* Edited by Heinz Kimmerle. Abhandlungen der Heidelberger Akademie der Wissenschaften, Philosophisch-historische Klasse, 1959:2. Heidelberg: Carl Winter Universitätverlag, 1959.

Schoeps, H.-J., and Benz, E. "Joachim Wach--In Memoriam." *Zeitschrift für Religions- und Geistesgeschichte,* IX (1957), pp. 368-374.

Schultz, Werner. "Die Grundlagen der Hermeneutik Schleiermachers, ihre Auswirkungen und ihre Grenzen." *Zeitschrift für Theologie und Kirche,* L (1953), pp. 158-184.

Schulz, Walter. *Wittgenstein: Die Negation der Philosophie.* Pfullingen: Günther Neske, 1967.

Séguy, Jean. "Expérience religieuse et sociologie des religions: Joachim Wach sociologue des religions." *Archives de sociologie des religions,* VII (1962), pp. 27-34.

Seiler, George Frederic. *Biblical Hermeneutics: or, the Art of Scripture Interpretation.* Translated by William Wright. London: Frederick Westley and A. H. Davis, 1835.

Senft, Christoph. "Die neue Aktualität Schleiermachers." *Philosophische Rundschau,* X (1962), pp. 283-290.

Smart, H. R. "Language-Games." *Philosophical Quarterly,* VII (1957), pp. 224-235.

Smith, Wilfred Cantwell. Review of *Types of Religious Experience: Christian and Non-Christian,* by Joachim Wach. *Journal of Religion,* XXXIII (1953), pp. 303-304

Specht, Ernst Konrad. *The Foundations of Wittgenstein's Late Philosophy.* Translated by D. E. Walford. Manchester: Manchester University Press, 1969.

Thulstrup, Niels. "An Observation Concerning Past and Present Hermeneutics." *Orbis Litterarum,* XXII (1967), pp. 24-44.

Toulmin, Stephen. "Ludwig Wittgenstein." *Encounter,* XXXII (1969), pp. 58-71.

Tuttle, Howard Nelson. *Wilhelm Dilthey's Philosophy of Historical Understanding: A Critical Analysis.* Leiden: E. J. Brill, 1969.

Wach, Joachim. "Bemerkungen zum Problem der 'externen' Würdigung der Religion." *Zeitschrift für Missionskunde und Religionswissenschaft,* XXXVIII (1923), pp. 161-183.

_____. *The Comparative Study of Religions.* Edited by Joseph M. Kitagawa. N.Y.: Columbia University Press, 1958.

_____. *Einführung in die Religionssoziologie.* Tübingen: J. C. B. Mohr (Paul Siebeck), 1931.

_____. *Der Erlösungsgedanke und seine Deutung.* Veröffentlichungen des Forschungsinstituts für vergleichende Religionsgeschichte an der Universität Leipzig, 8. Leipzig: J. C. Hinrichs, 1922.

_____. "Die Geschichtsphilosophie des 19. Jahrhunderts und die Theologie der Geschichte." *Historische Zeitschrift,* CXLII (1930), pp. 1-15.

_____. "Idee und Realität in der Religionsgeschichte." *Zeitschrift für Theologie und Kirche,* VII (1927), pp. 334-364.

_____. "The Interpretation of Sacred Books." *Journal of Biblical Literature,* LV (1936), pp. 59-63.

_____. *Mahayana, besonders in Hinblick auf das Saddharma-Pundarika-Sutra: Eine Untersuchung über die religionsgeschichtliche Bedeutung eines heiligen Textes der Buddhisten.* München-Neubiberg: Oskar Schloss Verlag, 1925.

_____. "Ein Meisterstück der vergleichenden Religionsforschung." *Die Christliche Welt,* XLV (1931), pp. 20-25.

_____. "'Nur.' Gedanken über den Psychologizismus." *Zeitschrift für Missionskunde und Religionswissenschaft,* XXXIX (1924), pp. 209-215.

_____. "On Teaching History of Religions." *Pro Regno Pro Sanctuario.* Edited by W. J. Kooiman and J. M. van Veen. Nijkerk: G. F. Callenbach, 1950.

_____. "On Understanding." *The Albert Schweitzer Jubilee Book.* Edited by A. A. Roback. Cambridge, Mass.: Sci-Art Publishers, [1946].

_____. "Religionswissenschaft." *Die Religion in Geschichte und Gegenwart,* 2nd ed., IV. Tübingen: J. C. B. Mohr (Paul Siebeck), 1930.

_____. *Religionswissenschaft: Prolegomena zu ihrer wissenschafts-theoretischen Grundlegung.* Leipzig: J. C. Hinrichs, 1924.

_____. "Das Religiöse Gefühl." *Das Problem der Kultur und*

die ärztliche Psychologie. Vorträge des Instituts
für Geschichte der Medizin an der Universität Leipzig, 4. Leipzig: Thieme, 1931.

_____. *Sociology of Religion.* Chicago: University of
Chicago Press, 1944.

_____. "Sociology of Religion." *Twentieth Century Soci-
ology.* Edited by Georges Gurvitch. N.Y.: Philosophical Library, 1945.

_____. *Die Typenlehre Trendelenburgs und ihr Einfluss auf
Dilthey: Eine philosophie- und geistesgeschichtliche
Studie.* Philosophie und Geschichte, 11. Tübingen:
J. C. B. Mohr (Paul Siebeck), 1926.

_____. *Types of Religious Experience: Christian and Non-
Christian.* Chicago: University of Chicago Press,
1951.

_____. "Und die Religionsgeschichte? Eine Auseinanderset-
zung mit D. Paul Althaus." *Zeitschrift für Systematische Theologie,* VI (1929), pp. 484-497.

_____. *Understanding and Believing: Essays by Joachim Wach.*
Edited by Joseph M. Kitagawa. N.Y.: Harper & Row,
1968.

_____. "Verstehen." *Die Religion in Geschichte und Gegen-
wart,* 2nd ed., V. Tübingen: J. C. B. Mohr (Paul
Siebeck), 1931.

_____. *Das Verstehen: Grundzüge einer Geschichte der her-
meneutischen Theorie im 19. Jahrhundert.* 3 vols.
Tübingen: J. C. B. Mohr (Paul Siebeck), 1926-33.

_____. "Wilhelm Dilthey über 'Das Problem der Religion.'"
*Zeitschrift für Missionskunde und Religionswissen-
schaft,* XL (1925), pp. 66-81.

_____. "Zur Beurteilung Friedrich Schlegels." *Philosophi-
scher Anzeiger,* IV (1929), pp. 13-26.

_____. "Zur Hermeneutik heiliger Schriften." *Theologische
Studien und Kritiken,* CII (1930), pp. 280-290.

_____. "Zur Methodologie der allgemeinen Religionswissen-
schaft." *Zeitschrift für Missionskunde und Religionswissenschaft,* XXXVIII (1923), pp. 33-55.

_____. Review of *Wilhelm Dilthey: An Introduction,* by H.
A. Hodges. *Journal of Religion,* XXVI (1946), pp.
74-75.

Waismann, Friedrich. *Wittgenstein und der Wiener Kreis.*
Edited by B. F. McGuinness. Oxford: Basil Blackwell, 1965.

Wisdom, John. "A Feature of Wittgenstein's Technique."

Paradox and Discovery. Oxford: Basil Blackwell, 1965.

Wittgenstein, Ludwig. "Bemerkungen über Frazers *The Golden Bough*." *Synthese*, XVII (1967), pp. 233-253.

_____. *Lectures and Conversations on Aesthetics, Psychology and Religious Belief*. Compiled from notes taken by Yorick Smythies, Rush Rhees and James Taylor. Edited by Cyril Barrett. Berkeley and Los Angeles: University of California Press, 1967.

_____. *Notebooks, 1914-1916*. Edited by G. H. von Wright and G. E. M. Anscombe. Translated by G. E. M. Anscombe. Oxford: Basil Blackwell, 1961.

_____. "Notes for Lectures on 'Private Experience' and 'Sense-Data.'" *Philosophical Review*, LXXVII (1968), pp. 275-320.

_____. *On Certainty*. Edited by G. E. M. Anscombe and G. H. von Wright. Translated by Denis Paul and G. E. M. Anscombe. Oxford: Basil Blackwell, 1969.

_____. *Philosophical Investigations*. 3rd ed. Edited by G. E. M. Anscombe and Rush Rhees. Translated by G. E. M. Anscombe. N.Y.: Macmillan Company, 1958.

_____. *Philosophische Bemerkungen*. Edited by Rush Rhees. Oxford: Basil Blackwell, 1965.

_____. *Philosophische Grammatik*. Edited by Rush Rhees. Oxford: Basil Blackwell, 1969.

_____. *Preliminary Studies for the "Philosophical Investigations" Generally Known as the Blue and Brown Books*. Edited by Rush Rhees. Oxford: Basil Blackwell, 1958.

_____. *Remarks on the Foundations of Mathematics*. Edited by G. H. von Wright, Rush Rhees, and G. E. M. Anscombe. Translated by G. E. M. Anscombe. Oxford: Basil Blackwell, 1964.

_____. *Tractatus Logico-Philosphicus*. Translated by D. F. Pears and B. F. McGuinness. London: Routledge & Kegan Paul, 1961.

_____. *Zettel*. Edited by G. E. M. Anscombe and G. H. von Wright. Translated by G. E. M. Anscombe. Oxford: Basil Blackwell, 1967.